CARL A. RUDISILL LIBRARY
LENOIR RHYNE COLLEGE

SO-BAR-194

The Romantic Tradition in American Literature

The Romantic Tradition
in American Literature

Advisory Editor

HAROLD BLOOM
Professor of English, Yale University

POEMS OF
SIXTY-FIVE YEARS

[WILLIAM] ELLERY CHANNING

SELECTED AND EDITED BY

F. B. SANBORN

ARNO PRESS

A NEW YORK TIMES COMPANY

New York • 1972

CARL A. RUDISILL LIBRARY
LENOIR RHYNE COLLEGE

811.2
C36P
96099
Feb. 1976

Reprint Edition 1972 by Arno Press Inc.

The Romantic Tradition in American Literature
ISBN for complete set: 0-405-04620-0
See last pages of this volume for titles.

Manufactured in the United States of America

ᑭᕋᑭᕋᑭᕋᑭᕋᑭᕋᑭᕋᑭᕋᑭᕋ

Library of Congress Cataloging in Publication Data

Channing, William Ellery, 1817-1901.
    Poems of sixty-five years.

    (The Romantic tradition in American literature)
    I. Title. II. Series.
PS1290.P8 1972   811'.2   72-4956
ISBN 0-405-04628-6

*This copy of " Poems of Sixty-five Years "
is one of an edition of three hundred
copies on Old Stratford paper and
fifteen copies on Japan vellum
paper, printed in April, nine-
teen hundred and two*

POEMS OF
SIXTY-FIVE YEARS

POEMS OF
SIXTY-FIVE YEARS

BY

ELLERY CHANNING

SELECTED AND EDITED BY

F. B. SANBORN

" If my bark sinks, 't is to another sea "

PHILADELPHIA AND CONCORD
JAMES H. BENTLEY
1902

Copyright, 1902, by
F. B. SANBORN OF CONCORD

THE DE VINNE PRESS

Dear Reader! if my verse could say
  How in my blood that Nature runs
Which manifesteth no decay—
    The fire that lights a thousand suns;
      How thou and I are freely lent
      A little of that element:

If I could say what landscape says,
  And human pictures say far more—
If I could twine the sunny days
    With the rich colors on the floor
      Of daily Love—how thou and I
      Might be refreshed with charity!

How grateful is the softened smile
  Of winter sunset o'er the snow!
And blessed is our spheral isle
    That through the unknown void must go;
      The current of that stream is sweet
      Where many waters closely meet.

The reader is indebted for this volume
to two friends of poesy and admirers
of Channing's verse, James H. Bentley
and Henry S. Borneman of Philadelphia, who in the summer of 1901 pro-
posed to Mr. Channing and the editor
the publication of such a volume at their
expense. The poet accepted the generous proposal, and the editor under-
took to make the selections, chiefly
from the published volumes. But by
the bequest of Mr. Channing he became
the owner of his manuscripts and
revised editions, and has made much
use of both those sources in this work.

F. B. S.

CONTENTS

ix

CONTENTS

CONTENTS

xi

BIOGRAPHICAL INTRODUCTION

FTER arrangements were made for the publication of this volume, with the approval of the poet, though without his active coöperation, and while the earlier poems were copying for its pages, he fell ill, at the age of a little more than eighty-three, and, with a confinement to his north-western chamber of but three weeks, passed from earth, with little suffering and no struggle—too soon to give his friends the publishers the pleasure of showing him this completed book. Yet this sad fact releases the editor from those restrictions of delicacy that would otherwise have checked his pen in writing the short biography which so secluded a poet must need in coming before the grandchildren of those who first welcomed his verses, in the years before 1840.

William Ellery Channing was born in Bedford Street, Boston, a few rods from the birthplace of Waldo Emerson, November 29, 1818. He was the son of Dr. Walter Channing, an eminent Boston physician, and of his first wife, Barbara Perkins, daughter of Samuel Gardiner Perkins, granddaughter of Stephen Higginson, and niece of Colonel Thomas H. Perkins, long the typical merchant prince of Boston. His mother dying early, Ellery was brought up for some years by his great-aunt Mrs. Bennett Forbes of Milton, mother of John M. Forbes, a later merchant prince of Boston. At an age earlier than boys usually go to such a school he was sent a hundred miles from home to the famous Round Hill School of Dr. Cogswell and George Bancroft (the future historian) at Northampton, where he remained three years, among boys generally much older than himself, of whom the historian Motley and Thomas Gold Appleton may be specially named. He completed his preparation for Harvard at the Boston schools, where the late William Maxwell Evarts and the celebrated surgeon Henry Bigelow were his companions; but studied for a time in the private school of Mr. Hubbard in Brookline, where for a few weeks in 1831 Charles Sumner

xiv

was one of his teachers. Entering at Harvard in the summer of 1834, a year after Henry Thoreau, and in the same class with James Russell Lowell and his own distant cousin Richard Henry Dana, Ellery Channing remained only a few months, and never rejoined his class. He spent much time at this period among his relatives and acquaintances at the romantic farm-house known as Curzon's Mill, in the angle formed by the Merrimac and its slender tributary the Artichoke River, four miles west of Newburyport; and this was a favorite resort of his in after years. Some of his early poems, printed by Emerson in 1840, describe the scenery of that region—particularly *The River*.

His earliest poem to be printed, however, came out in the *New England Magazine* of October, 1835, before he was seventeen years old, and without his knowledge, having been sent by a friend to Park Benjamin, then editing that Boston monthly. This poem, *The Spider*, in a favorite metre of Emerson's, appeared in Channing's first series of poems in 1843, and was one of the counts in the indictment which Lowell brought against Channing and Thoreau in his *Fable for Critics*. There is in it a remarkable vein of thought, glance of observation, and easy mastery of verse, which promised much for the maturity of so felicitous an author. Its publication in the last volume of this early Boston monthly (whose editor, Park Benjamin, in the following year transformed it into the *American Monthly Magazine*, issued in New York) brought Channing into the company of an older and more successful writer, Hawthorne. In that final issue of the *New England Magazine* Hawthorne had four tales and sketches, — *The Old Maid in the Winding-sheet, The Vision of the Fountain*, and *The Devil in Manuscript*, besides an account of the White Mountains and of canal-boating. But there was no acquaintance with the recluse Hawthorne until he married and took up his abode in the Old Manse, where he and Channing became close friends.

The Spider, when included by his friend Samuel Gray Ward in Channing's first series of poems (1843), varied but little from its first form, though shortened slightly. When, four years later, Emerson's first collection of poems came out, the resemblance in form of Channing's *Spider* to a favorite metre of Emerson led people to say that Channing had imitated Emerson's *Humblebee*, though in fact his poem was written and printed before a line of Emerson's verse had attracted notice.

As the work of a boy this poem is remarkable, and has a finish and melody which many of Channing's later verses lack. It appeared in the Boston monthly in this form :

BIOGRAPHICAL INTRODUCTION

Habitant of castle gray,
Creeping thing in sober way,
Visible sage mechanician,
Skilfulest arithmetician;
Aged animal at birth,
Wanting joy and idle mirth,
Clothed in famous tunic old,
Vestments black, of many a fold,
Spotted mightily with gold;
Weaving, spinning in the sun
Since the world its course has run.
Creation beautiful in art,
Of God's providence a part!
What if none will look at thee,
Sighing for the humming bee,
Or great moth with heavenly wings,
Or the nightingale who sings?
Curious spider! thou 'rt to me
Of a mighty family.

Tender of a mystic loom,
Spinning in my silent room
Canopy that haply vies
With the mortal fabric wise:
Everlasting procreator!
Ne'er was such a generator.

Adam wondered at thy skill
And thy persevering will,
That continueth to spin,
Caring not a yellow pin
For the mortal's dire confusion:
Sager in profound conclusion
Than astronomer at night
When he brings new worlds to light.
Heaven has furnished thee with tools
Such as ne'er a heap of fools
Have, by dint of sweat and pain,
Made for use—and made in vain.

When mild breeze is hither straying,
Sweetest music kindly playing,
Raising high the whispering leaves
And the covering of the sheaves,
Thou art rocking, airy thing!
Like a proud, exalted king:
Conqueror thou surely art,
And majestical of heart.

There are times of loneliness
When a living thing we bless—
Times of miserable sin,
Cold without and dark within:
Then, old spider, haply I
Seek thy busy factory;

BIOGRAPHICAL INTRODUCTION

Always finding thee at home,
Too forecasting e'er to roam.
So we sit and spin together,
In the gayest, gloomiest weather.

Here, in the volume of 1843, the poem ends; but
in the magazine it ran on thus:

Friends that come and go away
Now and then amuse a day,
But, for all sad times, gay seasons,
And intelligible reasons,
Comrades, spinning in the sun,
We will this existence run;
Brothers we, by God connected,
Ne'er with bitterness infected;
So, when ends this mortal life,
We, with joy and goodness rife,
Shall wing the air to happiness
And everlasting blessedness.

The success of this early poem seems to have
fixed Ellery Channing's determination to devote
himself to literature in the poetic form. In 1847,
when, without an outward vocation, a place was
offered him as journalist in a well-established Boston
newspaper, he declined it without hesitation, saying to a friend in Concord: "I told them that, by
the grace of God, I would never desert the Muse

any more, place or no place, poor or rich; that I would stick fast to her; and that there should be at least one professional poet left. Twelve years it has cost me to get here, and what remains shall go the same road." By this calculation he had begun to count himself a professional poet as early as 1835.

In the meantime he neglected few opportunities to gain that knowledge of Nature and the human conditions which every poet needs. It may have been the mere restlessness of youth, and the moods of a character essentially capricious, which first kept him from settling down to any of the customary pursuits of Bostonians in his inherited station of life; but it was a poetic instinct which drew him to the wild and lovely aspects of Nature and the abodes of unconventional men. As a youth he was familiar with the mountain scenery of New Hampshire, and with the solitudes of the sea-coast and the capes; and he spent whole days and nights in places remote from the haunts of men or even the frequent visitation of tourists. Traces of this outdoor life appear everywhere in his verse, as does his early bent toward the life of a painter—a tendency encouraged by his intimacy with Washington Allston, who had married his aunt Miss Channing, and, after her death, had wedded a distant cousin of his through the Ellerys, Miss Dana of Cambridge. It

was also heightened by his early friendship for Mr.
Ward, in whom the artistic instinct was very strong.
The next poem which I find dated among his
papers is one that I published for him in the *Boston
Commonwealth* in 1863 under the title of *Newbury
Hills,* but which was written in 1836, and then called
Byfield Hills—Byfield being a district in Old New-
bury (not yet Newburyport), within easy reach of
Curzon's Mill and the Artichoke stream. The two
charming poems relating to this stream, *The River*
and *Isabel,* date back to 1836–37 ; and, indeed, many
of the verses in the collection of 1840 must have
been written before the poet migrated to northern
Illinois in 1839. He settled with a friend, Joseph
Dwight, a cousin of his Berkshire kinsmen the
Sedgewicks, in McHenry County, west of Lake
County and bordering on the rolling prairies of
Wisconsin ; and there, after testing the solitude
of the country, he bought a hundred and sixty
acres of land in what was then Hartland township,
four miles from the present city of Woodstock—of
which eighty acres was woodland. The seller was
Franklin Griffing, the date of purchase was November 9, 1839, and it was sold by the young pioneer
to Pliny Hayward, a Massachusetts man, October
22, 1840 ; soon after which the poet took up his
abode for a year or two in Cincinnati, where his
maternal uncle Rev. James H. Perkins had a parish

for a few years. There Mr. Channing taught pupils
and studied law—the latter in a desultory way, as
he had studied medicine with his father in Boston.
But he made many friends in Cincinnati,—forming
the acquaintance of the Longworth, Blackwell, and
Cranch families, and many more,—wrote for the
newspapers (as he had done in Boston before
going West), and enjoyed the agreeable society.
There he fell in love with Miss Ellen Fuller, a
younger sister of Margaret the sibylline, and married her in the autumn of 1842—having in the
meantime become one of the regular contributors
to the *Dial* of Margaret Fuller, Emerson, and George
Ripley. Naturally, therefore, when he returned to
the East he sought. after a brief residence in Cambridge near his uncle Professor Edward Channing,
and his cousins the Danas, to establish himself in
the vicinity of Emerson. Writing to him years
afterward, Ellery Channing said :

> I have but one reason for settling in one place
> in America : it is because you are there. I not
> only have no preference for any place, but I do
> not know that I should be able to settle upon
> any place if you were not living. I came to
> Concord attracted by you, because your mind,
> your talents, your cultivation, are superior to
> those of any man I know, living or dead. I

incline to go where the man is, or where the men are, just as naturally as I should sit by the fire in the winter. The men are the fire in this great winter of humanity.

At his first residence in Concord, where he had visited Emerson before, Ellery Channing established himself in a cottage on the Cambridge turnpike, almost adjoining the estate of Emerson, and there he was living when his intimate friend Ward assumed the cost of printing his first volume of poems, in the spring or summer of 1843. Most of the verses in this book of a hundred and sixty pages had been written some years earlier; some of them, like the *Song of the Earth-Spirit*, were parts of longer poems; others had been printed in the *Dial*.

Before July, 1840, when the first quarterly number of the *Dial* was issued, his friends had placed in Emerson's hands a collection of Channing's early poems, a list of which, from his own early handwriting, follows. I have indicated which of them have not been printed, so far as known, up to this time, when a few of those unpublished appear in this volume.

Sunday Poem. (Nine parts, 8 pages.)	Sea-Song.
	Our Birthdays.
A Song of Spring.	For a Wood Scene in Winter.
Alek. (Printed as "Arab Song.")	The Harbor. (Unprinted.)
	October.

POEMS OF SIXTY-FIVE YEARS

After reading these poems in manuscript, Emerson wrote an essay for the October *Dial* (1840) on *New Poetry*, in which he published several of Channing's pieces, with these introductory comments:

We have fancied that we drew greater pleasure from some manuscript verses than from

printed ones of equal talent. For there was
herein the charm of character; they were con-
fessions; and the faults, the imperfect parts, the
fragmentary verses, the halting rhymes, had a
worth beyond that of a high finish. They testi-
fied that the writer was more man than artist,
more earnest than vain; that the thought was
too sweet and sacred to him than that he should
suffer his ears to hear or his eyes to see a superficial defect in the expression. If poetry of this
kind has merit, we conceive that the prescrip-
tion which demands a rhythmical polish may be
easily set aside; and when a writer has out-
grown the state of thought which produced the
poem, the interest of letters is served by publish-
ing it imperfect, as we preserve studies, torsos,
and blocked statues of the great masters.

Here is poetry which asks no aid of magni-
tude or number, of blood or crime, but finds
theatre enough in the first field or brookside,
breadth and depth enough in the flow of its own
thought. Here is self-repose which to our mind
is stabler than the Pyramids. Here is self-respect
which leads a man to date from his own heart
more proudly than from Rome. Here is love
which sees through surface and adores the gentle
nature and not the costume. Here is the good
wise heart which sees that the end of culture is

strength and cheerfulness. Here is poetry more
purely intellectual than any American verses
we have yet seen, distinguished from all com-
petition by two merits—the fineness of perception, and the poet's trust in his own genius
to that degree that there is an absence of all
conventional imagery. The writer was not
afraid to write ill; he had a great meaning too
much at heart to stand for trifles, and wrote
lordly for his peers alone.

A whole generation later, in 1871, when I carried
him the manuscript of Channing's *Wanderer*, whose
title I had suggested, and procured from Emerson
a preface to this fifth volume of his friend's poetry,
he confirmed his early verdict with even stronger
praise, saying:

Here is Hamlet in the fields, with never a
thought to waste even on Horatio's opinion of
his sallies. Plainly the author is a man of large
reading in a wide variety of studies; but his
books have not tamed his invincible personality.
His interest in nature is not pedantic, much less
culinary—but insatiably curious of the hint it
gives of its cause, and its relation to man. All
his use of it is free and searching. This book
requires a good reader, a lover and inquirer of

nature; and such a one will find himself re-
warded. If there is neglect of conventional
ornament and correct finish which even looks a
little studied,—as if the poet crippled his pen-
tameters to challenge notice of a subtler melody,
—yet here are strokes of skill which recall the
great masters. Here is the mountain truly pictured : the upland day, the upland night, the
perpetual home of the wind ; every hint of the
primeval agencies noted, and the thoughts which
these bring to youth and to maturity. The book
is written to himself—is his forest or street experience, the record of his moods, fancies, observations, and studies, and will interest good
readers as such. He will write,—as he has ever
written,—whether he has readers or not. But
his poems have to me and others an exceptional
value for this reason : we have not been con-
sidered in their composition, but either defied
or forgotten ; and therefore we consult them
freely as photographs.

The sentences of this matchless critic have here
been brought together because they touch their
subject with so fine and so generous an appreciation ; but between the portfolio of 1840 and the sheets
of *The Wanderer* there was intercalated a long suc-
cession of experiences and poetic endeavors. In

1847 Channing published a second series of poems; in 1849 a third, entitled *The Woodman;* in 1858 a single poem, precursor of *The Wanderer*, which he called *Near Home*, though it described two of his dearest haunts—the Concord woods and river-meadows, and the Atlantic sea-coast of Massachusetts; and at intervals occasional poems for special events —the consecration of the Sleepy Hollow cemetery, the funeral of Henry Thoreau, the centenary of Bronson Alcott's native town in Connecticut, and the birthdays and weddings of his near friends. In 1873 he revised and enlarged an earlier-written biography of Thoreau, and published it with *Memorial Verses* annexed. To most of these volumes and brochures the public paid very slight attention; the copies were returned on his hands unsold, like the greater part of Thoreau's first edition of the *Week;* nor did he attempt, as Thoreau did, to amend their sale by dealing in them himself. On the contrary, he philosophically cut up the unbound sheets of his *Conversations in Rome* (1847), and upon their blank spaces wrote those remarkable poems describing Cape Cod, and afterward his life of Thoreau. This was not exactly seething the kid in its mother's milk, which was forbidden to the Jews; nor was it making one hand wash the other, according to our proverb: but it was something between the two.

Quite as varied were his worldly experiences.

In 1844 he was induced to go to New York and help
Horace Greeley, George Ripley, and Margaret Fuller
edit the *Tribune;* in 1845 he crossed the Atlantic in
a Mediterranean packet and spent a few months in
France and Italy. In the years following his unsuc-
cessful volumes of verse he tried his fortune at
lecturing in half a dozen New England cities and
towns—Boston, Providence, Plymouth, Worcester,
etc. He joined Thoreau in some of his tours—
among the Berkshire Hills, along Cape Cod, in some
New Hampshire rambles, and through French Canada. Earlier, during Hawthorne's abode in the Old
Manse, which his genius immortalized, Channing
took him on excursions in Thoreau's Merrimac boat
upon the Concord and the Assabet rivers, and in
many a walk to scenes of picturesque beauty.

Thoreau himself had early become intimate with
his new neighbor, read the poems of 1843 with
appreciation, and wrote from Staten Island to
Emerson, in May of that year: "Tell Channing I
saw a man buy a copy at Little & Brown's; he may
have been a virtuoso, but we will give him the
credit." And again, in July: "Tell him to remain
at least long enough to establish Concord's right and
interest in him. I was beginning to know the
man." Indeed, Channing did remain in Concord,
with occasional absences, until he had seen the
funerals of all his literary friends of the earlier

period : Thoreau's in 1862, Hawthorne's in 1864,
Mrs. Ripley's in 1867, Emerson's in 1882, and Alcott's and Louisa's in 1888.

Thoreau, who had quoted his verses in the *Week*,
and again in *Walden* (in 1854), had this to say of
Channing in that most popular of his volumes :

> The one who came from farthest to my lodge,
> through deepest snows and most dismal tem-
> pests, was a poet. A farmer, a hunter, a soldier,
> a reporter, even a philosopher, may be daunted,
> but nothing can deter a poet, for he is actuated
> by pure love. Who can predict his comings and
> goings? His business calls him out at all hours,
> even when doctors sleep. We made that small
> house ring with boisterous mirth and resound
> with the murmur of much sober talk. At suit-
> able intervals there were regular salutes of laugh-
> ter, which might have been referred indiffer-
> ently to the last uttered or the forthcoming jest.

This implies what has been the constant fact of
Ellery Channing's life, in spite of the melancholy
shadowed forth in his verse—a lively and humorous
turn of mind, with sallies of merriment, which dis-
tinguish his letters as much as his conversation—
perhaps more. He did not spare his friends in his
grotesque observations, and, in spite of his respect
and admiration for Bronson Alcott, could not help

satirizing him. Thus in November, 1847, after Emerson had sailed for England, and Thoreau had migrated from his Walden lodge to take Emerson's place in the household, Channing wrote to his absent friend thus concerning the celebrated arbor or garden cell which Alcott, with much labor and good taste, was building on Emerson's lawn :

> Now for the summer-house, that all-important feature. You know to what I refer—the chapel of ease which our great philosopher is erecting on the lawn ; is erecting and has been erecting. There it is, or the idea of it. This eternal pancake, which not even the all-powerful rays of the Alcott sun have quite baked, has finally drawn on its double nightcap. First a wickerwork skull ; then a head of moss, affirmed by those who have seen it to be admirable ; lastly, a straw nightcap. Even the thermometer at sixteen below zero cannot pinch its ears. In other words, the building of this microscopic Cathedral of Cologne realizes eternity. Tantalus's occupation 's gone. Our ancient has his meals brought there, works from morning till night, and dreams (so Mrs. A. affirms) about this Tom Thumb of a St. Peter's.

Between Emerson's return home in 1848 and my arrival in Concord early in 1855, a plan had been formed for a combined series of walks and talks, in which Emerson, Thoreau, Channing, and perhaps Alcott, were to take part, and a volume made up from them which Channing was to edit. It involved copying from the journals of these intimate friends, as well as actual conversations reported by Channing; and was faithfully elaborated by him into the form of a book, to be published with or without the names of the talkers, as might be judged best. The plan was never carried out; but a dozen years later, or nearer twenty, when printing his life of Thoreau, Channing inserted therein some pages from this manuscript, including passages from Emerson's and Thoreau's journals, and even a few verses of Emerson's which had not elsewhere been printed at that time.

Few of our authors have ever written on so persistently with so little evidence of popular approval. His only really popular book was his life of Thoreau, published in 1873, thirty years after the venture of his first volume of verse, which was made up in part from his contributions to the *Dial*, where Emerson and Margaret Fuller welcomed him as a contributor before he was two-and-twenty.

He worked for a time under Horace Greeley in the New York *Tribune*, and he afterward for a year or two helped edit the New Bedford *Mercury;* but he adhered to his early vow, and was a professional

xxxii

poet all his days. Since his death I have found on
his table what I take to be his last poem, addressed
to the daughter of a friend, not then two years old ;
and it shows the same charms and the same faults
that his verses had sixty-six years ago, when the
first one was printed.

TO MARJORIE—DREAMING

We must not weep, we will not moan ;
Let all such things be deemed unknown.
Now for the words of livelong hope
In Marjorie's white horoscope !

Good-by to all that dims our eyes—
Welcome her, kind futurities !
Anthems of joy and hymns of gold—
All these let Marjorie infold !

Yes, for that sweet and peaceful child,
That gift of beauty undefiled,
A smile of love, a song of joy,
Shall Marjorie's dream of life employ.

I see the sunset o'er the hill,
The level meads with glory fill—
A gentle light, a heavenly balm,
Like Marjorie's soul, so clear and calm.

xxxiii

This last stanza has an affecting interest; it was
from his windows overlooking the river-meadows
and the moorland around Nashawtuc that he daily
watched the landscape and nightly observed the
silent march of the stars. Such were the scenes his
artist-nature loved to view—and to how many of
our quiet nooks of rural beauty has he conducted
me and scores of his friends! That was his special
talent as a walker, remembered by all who ever
strolled with him, and particularly commemorated
by Emerson and by Hawthorne. In Emerson's
diary occurs this passage—one of several in which
he praises the social gifts of Ellery Channing:

Another walk with Ellery Channing, well worth
commemoration, if that were possible; but no
pen could write what we saw. Ellery found,
as usual, the place where your house should
be set,— with excellent judgment,— leaving
the wood-paths as they were, which no art
could make over. After leaving White Pond
we struck across an orchard to a steep hill of
the right New Hampshire slope, and came pres-
ently into rudest woodland landscapes, unknown,
undescribed, and hitherto unwalked by us Satur-
day afternoon professors. Ellery said he had
once fancied that there were some amateur
trades (as politics), but he found there were

none; these, too, were fenced by Whig barri-
cades. Even walking could not be done by
amateurs, but by professors only. In walking
with Ellery you shall always see what was never
before shown to the eye of man.

These walks were with many friends, and were
long continued. They began in Concord, with
Emerson, as early as 1841; with Thoreau and Hawthorne a little later; with all three they ended only
with their lifetime, or the enfeebled health that
preceded death. Channing had even arranged to
join Thoreau at Niagara, and make with him that
last long journey of his to Minnesota and the homes
of the Sioux in 1861; but when the time came, the
poet's sensitive heart failed him. With Hawthorne
he sailed and rowed about the two rivers of Concord
in Thoreau's Merrimac boat; and in his *Mosses* the
novelist has commemorated those short voyages.
With Alcott he walked but little; that philosopher,
though a stalwart figure, cared less for walks than
for conversation. For myself, I have rambled thou-
sands of miles with Channing during the nearly
forty-seven years of our friendship, and he has
made me acquainted with every nook of picturesque beauty and every wide-reaching view in this
lovely region, so much like English Warwickshire.
Along with this artist-eye and poet's imagination

went a mingling of intellectual and moral traits
hard to define. Conscience and whim, duty and
caprice, were strangely intermixed and transfused;
so that something which would strike another man
—say Thoreau—as an obligation, might seem to
Channing but a dream of possibility. Struck with
this trait, Thoreau, recording one walk fifty years
ago, made this acute observation, which is still the
best account that I know:

In our walks, Channing takes out his note-book
sometimes, and tries to write as I do—but all
in vain. He soon puts it up again, or contents
himself with scrawling some sketch of the landscape. Observing me still scribbling, he will
say that he confines himself to the ideal—purely
ideal remarks; he leaves the facts to me. Sometimes, too, he will say, a little petulantly: 'I am
universal; I have nothing to do with the particular and definite.' He is the moodiest person,
perhaps, that I ever saw; as naturally whimsical
as a cow is brindled. Both in his tenderness
and his roughness he belies himself. He can be
incredibly selfish and unexpectedly generous.
He is conceited—and yet there is in him
far more than usual to ground conceit upon.
He is one who will not stoop to rise. He
wants something for which he will not pay the

going price. He will only learn slowly by failure.

Failure and success indeed came to him in his long and by no means idle life; but the worldly failure was out of proportion to the worldly success. He bore them both with a real fortitude which was only the more pronounced because of the superficial petulance and impatience he so often displayed.

What Channing's view was of Thoreau's writing habit, and his interest in outward Nature, may be learned from an entry in his journal of March, 1867, five years after Thoreau's death. Channing was then engaged in writing or revising his life of Thoreau, which did not finally appear until 1873. Thus runs the journal:

Henry was fond of making an ado, a wonder, a surprise of all facts that took place out of doors; but a picture, a piece of music, a novel, did not affect him in that fashion. He exaggerated the permanence of everything but what men do; and, like all writers who have had literary success, he necessarily deemed his own writing of special importance. It is well that some fail, or none would know what a trifle the best writing is. But this trait of exaggeration in Henry was as pleasing as possible, so far as his companion

was concerned. Nothing was more delightful
than the enormous curiosity, the continued
greenness, the effervescing wonder of this child
of Nature—glad of everything its mother
said or did. This joy in Nature is something
we can get over, like love. And yet, love—
that is a hard toy to smash and to fling under
the grate for good. Now, Henry made no account
of love at all, apparently. He had notions
about friendship. I have always been surprised
at the pertinacity with which Henry kept to
the writing of his journals. This was something
truly heroic. I should have fancied his thoughts
would have run out; that the stream would
have become dry. But there are the 30 volumes, all done in ten years; besides all the
other writing,—and no little, truly,—that he
must have done in the same period.

Thoreau surely had a certain "literary success"
in his lifetime, and much more since; while his
companion in the walks regarded his own failure
as complete. The genius Channing inherited was
improved by study and experience, but its literary
expression gained little in comparison with the
wisdom that lay behind it. Failure had given him
a juster estimate of himself, and had not injured
his mind or his morals by the poison of envy, that
disappointment so often infuses in hearts as sus-

ceptible. It was this very susceptibility that made him often seem distant or harsh; the wounds of time, the sharp changes and reverses of life, fell upon his tender heart with the insufferable keenness of physical pain; and he must withdraw into himself till the hurt had partly healed. His true friends were those who did not exact or even expect from him what might be required of an ordinary acquaintance. In the years that I have known him familiarly, though much was seen which I would have changed had change been possible, I ever found him worthy of friendship.

In explanation of the contradictions in our poet's nature, which all who knew him intimately saw, and by which strangers might be either strongly attracted or sharply repelled. a few words may be said. His mother dying too early to give him a mother's care, he never knew in boyhood what it was to have the atmosphere of a happy home about him. A sensitive nature turned this deprivation into a source of melancholy in extreme youth, on which he often dwelt in his earlier and sadder poems. In one of these, written before he was of age, and never before printed, he said:

I tell you, sudden fates which come to me,
   Ye are not faithful! Hear: my mother died
Before I clasped her, and that parent's knee
   Me never knew—my tears she never dried;

But with the unknown upward then I grew,
Far from all that which was to me most true.

    That early life was bitter oft;
      And like a flower whose roots are dry
    I withered; for my feelings soft
      Were by my brothers passèd by.
        Storm-wind fell on me,
        Dark clouds lowered on me;
    Many ghosts swept trembling past;
    Cold looks in my eyes they cast.

Upon this sad mood—by no means unusual in those of a poetic temperament—there came the gladdening presence of outward Nature; and the verse goes on:

    Then spoke the Spirit of the Earth,
      Her gentle voice like gliding water's song:
    "None from my loins have ever birth
      But they to joy and love belong;
    I faithful am, and give to thee
    Blessings great—and give them free."

From that early day Ellery Channing became the poet of outward Nature and inward sensibility—too keenly alive to all that vibrates in the chords of feeling to pursue or even accept the routine of dis-

cipline; but also too perceptive of all the shows of
Nature not to delineate them well in such verse
as the Muse gave him. This was often magical in
single lines or whole stanzas, but something ren-
dered him little capable of revising and polishing;
so that what Emerson said of Alcott was just as true
of Channing: "A little finish and articulation
added to his potencies, and he would have com-
pared with the greatest." Concerning Channing
and his verses his friends remained steadily of the
same mind, as we have seen in Emerson's case; the
failure of the public to appreciate, and of the poet
to finish and clarify, did not affect their good opinion. When he was leaving Concord temporarily
for New Bedford, in 1855–56, and had formed a
new friendship with one of the New Bedford Quak-
ers, Daniel Ricketson, Thoreau wrote to the latter
(March, 1856):

I was surprised to hear that Channing was in
N. When he was here last, in December, he
said, like himself, that he "did not know the
name of the place where he lived." How to
serve him most effectually has long been a prob-
lem with his friends. Perhaps it is left for you
to solve it. I suspect that the most that you or
any one can do for him is to appreciate his
genius—to buy and read, and cause others to

buy and read, his poems. That is the hand he
has put forth to the world; take hold of that.
Your knowledge of Cowper will help you to
know Channing. He will accept sympathy and
aid, but he will not bear questioning. He will
ever be reserved and enigmatic, and you must
deal with him at arm's-length. I have no secrets to tell you concerning him, and do not wish
to call obvious excellences and defects by far-
fetched names. Nor need I suggest how witty
and poetic he is—and what an inexhaustible
fund of good-fellowship you will find in him.

Equally exhaustless, as years went by, became
Channing's fund of genial and exact learning in the
greatest variety of topics. An artist by nature, he
explored in his dusty chamber, or in the alcoves and
galleries of cities, the whole field of ancient and
modern art; and his verdict on painters, sculptors,
engravers, architects, decorators, etc., if capricious,
was sure to be memorable. Fond of travel and ad-
venture, yet shrinking from their inevitable conditions, he became an explorer by reading the books
and poring over the maps of others; and when I
was first in Greece, he astonished me, well as I had
known him, by his intimate knowledge of every
English and French scholar or virtuoso who had
searched out the lovely ruins of antiquity. The

authorship of *Junius*, the mystery of Mary of Scotland, and the Man in the Iron Mask, had no secrets from him ; he was equally at home in arctic voyages and with the forests and gorillas and lions of Africa. Medicine and surgery, botany and bird-lore, geology and the attractive alphabet of gems and precious metals, found him an eager and capable student. It is only needful to read his later poems, such as *The Wanderer*, and the heterogeneous resources of his *Thoreau*, to see from what distant and rich reservoirs his allusions and illustrations were drawn. As in his early poems he was often overwhelmed by the tide of his crowding fancies, so in later verses his stores of memory would hurry imagination on from point to point in bewildering caprice ; but the thick forest of his thought was ever traversed, here and there, by the silvery and glancing stream of poesy, as the mountain brook glides through the plane-trees of Ikaria in the gorges of Attica.

Ellery Channing was frugally supported in the latter half of his long life by a modest inherited income, which he sometimes increased by literary work, and from which he gave freely, in his own way, to those who needed aid or whose studies he chose to assist. Simple almost to asceticism in his own habits, living often on one meal a day, and making his wardrobe last beyond the hopes of his friends, he yet had the feelings and principles of a man of fortune, along with the austere geniality of an ancient philosopher. Next to fields and woods, skies and landscapes, his delight was in theatres and libraries; and few could discuss better the stage of two centuries, or the famous collections of scholars and artists, from the period of Babylonian cylinders to ours of the newspaper and the photograph. This made his conversation delightful when his darker moods or physical ills did not keep him silent. His last illness was brief and with little acute suffering, and he died quietly, at early morning, December 23, 1901—the last of the illustrious Concord brotherhood.

A few of his contemporaries, and the children and grandchildren of himself and his friends, assembled in the village church of Concord, the day after Christmas, to pay their last tribute of affection and neighborly regard to one of the oldest citizens of Concord, who made the town his residence from choice, and not by the accident of birth, and who returned to it more than once when accident or duty called him away. His life was quiet and almost unknown to the mass of his townsfolk; he added nothing to their burdens or their animosities, and little to their gossip; his duties to his companions or to those who served him were silently performed; he chose a recluse life, not from misanthropy, but because his constitution admitted no other; and he

was well described, twenty years before his birth,
by the English poet he admired :

> He is retired as noontide dew,
>   Or fountain in a noonday grove;
> And you must love him ere to you
> He will seem worthy of your love.
>
> In common things that round us lie
>   Some random truths he can impart—
> The harvest of a quiet eye,
>   That broods and sleeps on his own heart.

The portrait prefixed to this volume is one which
was taken about 1875, and nothing could better
present the cheerful and thoughtful dignity of his
middle life. An earlier portrait, painted by one of
the Cranch family about 1842, exists, and may be
engraved hereafter; but the man here represented
was he who wrote *The Wanderer* and *Thoreau the
Poet-Naturalist*, and who, at Emerson's request a
few years earlier, had written of the woodland ridges
where he is buried :

> Here shalt thou pause to hear the funeral bell
>   Slow stealing o'er thy heart in this calm place;
> Not with a throb of pain, a feverish knell,
>   But in its kind and supplicating grace
> It says: "Go, Pilgrim, on thy march ! be more
> Friend to the friendless than thou wast before."

POEMS OF SIXTY-FIVE YEARS

In selecting the poems for this edition the embarrassment of the editor has not been what to take, but what to omit; for the mass of verse written by this industrious poet, with very little encouragement from his readers, during the sixty-seven years that he was writing good verse, is far greater than he or his most partial friends would ever print. In one thick volume of manuscript containing a hundred and twenty-eight separate poems, written between 1848 and 1854, and carefully indexed, Channing had afterward inscribed on the fly-leaf, for my instruction: "No poem in this volume deserves publication—a truly sweeping remark, which the posthumous editor is requested to observe, within the proper conditions." Yet among these several have been printed and much quoted—*Baker Farm*, for instance, and *The Flight of Wild Geese*, of which Emerson had so high an opinion that he reserved it for *Parnassus* during many years. But these verses all have a biographic value, and contain hundreds of lines that would make the fortune of a modern poet if he could weave them skilfully into popular metres.

Apart from such compositions, which were exercises rather than poems, Channing wrote well-tuned verse enough to fill six or eight volumes; and he had success in many metres, as this volume will show to those who know what metrical success in

English verse is. With all this variety, and with a true poet's eye, which no feature of natural beauty and no trait of human nature escaped, Channing would use a few poetic words over and over, until the reader almost accused this imaginative and vocabulistic scholar of poverty in language. "Soft," "gentle," "air," "gray," "dim," "deep," "cold," "art," "heart," and a score of other words, inestimable in worth to a poet, but to be used sparingly and in varied connections, adorn or disfigure his fine passages—simply because he would not take the pains that revision of inspired verse usually requires. This fault, and another into which most poets fall,—of writing too much,—often weary the reader who is at first delighted with the fresh originality of the thought and the magical effect of the best lines. In both these defects he resembled the Elizabethan poets, and was not so far from the lyric passages of Greek poesy as those are apt to think who seize on its striking beauties, and are blind to its vague and darkling significance, even in some of the grandest passages. It would be a fine jest to turn a few of Channing's most enigmatic pages into Pindaric Greek, and bring them before the learned as newly found fragments of Alkman, Bacchylides, or Aeschylus; not one scholar in ten would suspect the fraud, and hundreds of learned essays would be expended on them in all the tongues of Europe.

What must strike every good reader of Channing's verse is the ease and grace with which he rises into great rhythms or sinks into pretty trifles and the very simplicity of fanciful childhood. Lines and whole pages might be ascribed to Marlowe or Johnson, Fletcher or Donne, and, more rarely, to Shakspeare; and few would detect the dissimilarity. Was it Marston who denounced

> Those worst virtues that the cozening world
> Pimps on her half-fledged brood; old shells and
>   worms
> That saw ere deluged Noah at the plough!

Or what Elizabethan was it who described

> The listening city or the landward town
> That spots afar the toppling mountain's base!

Did Ben Jonson say of Venetia Stanley:

> Rose on her cheeks, are roses in her heart,
> And softer on the earth her footstep falls
> Than earliest twilight airs across the wave!

Or was it Crashaw or Fanshaw or Beaumont or Herrick who wrote:

BIOGRAPHICAL INTRODUCTION

Some dry uprooted saplings we have seen
Pretend to even this grove of Heaven,
This sacred forest, where the foliage green
Breathes music like mild lutes, or silver-
coated flutes,
On the concealing winds, that can convey
Never their tone to the rude ear of day?

O. si sic omnia! But Channing had all the defects
of his qualities. The poetic temperament, almost
ignored or forgotten in this age, when everybody
writes verse and few write it well, ran in him to
its most capricious and traditional extremes. He
would have been more appreciated in the era of
Drayton and Spenser ; like them, he was a poets' poet,

And such fine madness he did still retain
As rightly should possess a poet's brain.

As a new edition of *Thoreau the Poet-Naturalist* is
soon to appear in Boston, containing the *Memorial
Poems,* which in Channing's mind were associated
with his dear friend Thoreau, all these are omitted
from this collection ; but some will be added in that
volume which have relation to the intimacy of
the two friends.

F. B. S.

CONCORD, MASSACHUSETTS,
February 1, 1902.

xlix

EARLY POEMS OF
ELLERY CHANNING

For the earliest known poem, *The Spider*,
see pages xvii-xix

THE BYFIELD HILLS

(1836)

THERE is a range of little barren hills,
  Skirting a dark and purely idle stream,
  Which winds among the fields, as in a dream
Of weary man a heavy sorrow rills
The down-prest spirit; whoso buildeth mills
  To break the grain on it? Yet never deem
  These barren little hills low as they seem—
They draw away from us a host of ills.

A lone flat rock is sleeping at its ease
  Upon their topmost line, beneath a wind
That oozes from the sea, nor touches trees
  In that bare spot, but murmurs to the mind
A misty tune of gray felicities—
  Salt Ocean's heart, thy pulse is strangely kind!

POEMS OF SIXTY-FIVE YEARS

SUNDAY POEM

This is the strange title given in the author's manuscript to a long auto-
biographical poem dwelling on the sadness of the poet's childish life,
the loss of an early love (a subject to which he often recurred, as will
be seen), and the consolation that he drew from the beauties and protec-
tions of Nature — here typified under the Goethean name of *The Earth-
Spirit*. This latter part was printed in 1843 as *The Earth-Spirit*, but
without this weird, pathetic introduction. A portion of the unprinted
lines are omitted.

I

ONWARD we float along the way
   Like straws upon a rapid river.
Changeth the weather every day;
   So change our human feelings ever—
     Yes, most of them thus change,
     And have a wider range,
   But there are those no time can sever.

Withers not the sun, my love!
   What of thee is mortal now
That was framed in worlds above;
   Thy full-thoughted archèd brow,
And the light of those clear eyes,
Death and change and Time defies.

The immortal there hath place,
   Gladly sits upon thy frame,
Lurketh in thy sunny face,
   In a wildness none can tame.

4

SUNDAY POEM

II

Away! the night is dark and drear;
 Loud howls the storm, the clouds uproar,
And chill as broken love the atmosphere.
 Away! thee, Nature, I can woo no more:
 Thou art at war, and naught at rest;
 With thee I never can be blest.

Thy whirling seas my feelings jar,
 Thy weeping winds and twilight cold;
Thy ways my seekings idly mar,
 And I was in my youth-time old.
 Thou didst set a glowing stone
 In a golden belt alone,—
To me thou sayest: "This treasure thine—
It is the richest thing of mine."

III

I stood amazed; my blood o'erran
 Its usual channels, till my veins
Would burst; I was again a man;
 Ending was here of all those pains—
Those cold, chill pains that crept about my way,
Those hidden shadows in the light of Day.
 What! no more of them to see!
 Chains were off and roaming free!

Then cried I to the corners of the Earth:
"It cannot be—ye mock at my despair!
For I was destined from my earliest birth
 To be beloved by nothing sweet or fair:
 And I have made my bed, and now am heir
To all that blackens and has naught of mirth.

"I tell you, sudden fates which come to me,
 Ye are not faithful! Hear: my mother died
Before I clasped her, and that parent's knee
 Me never knew—my tears she never dried;
But with the unknown upward then I grew,
Far from all that which was to me most true."

  That early life was bitter oft;
   And like a flower whose roots are dry
  I withered; for my feelings soft
   Were by my brothers passèd by.
    Storm-wind fell on me,
    Dark clouds lowered on me;
  Many ghosts swept trembling past;
  Cold looks in my eyes they cast.

IV

Older I grew then, but I was not more
 Joy's child than in those earlier, other hours;
It was the same unyielding penance o'er.
 My crown was not of thorns, but withered flowers,

6

SUNDAY POEM

Dry buds, and half blown roses dry with dust;
Thorns had been glorious, glorious by their side,
For in their frantic pain there rises trust,
While these are phantoms of what may have died.
    I see ye still around me;
      Why is it said! To sadden!
     That there is some joy for me!
     Ah! think you me to gladden!

Sang the voice sweetly: "We say what we say;
There is joy in thy cup, there is sun in thy day."
I groaned aloud: "Alas, they mock!
Stood other form in other years,—
    Her song,—then came the lightning's shock,
And the sharp fire of those wild tears;
I carry them within, on many biers.
I stand like one who came to sing with those
That sang so sweetly, all of love and joy;
Their voices yet!—while I am hung with woes;
Life comes to me, yet comes but to destroy."

V

Then spoke the Spirit of the Earth,
    Her gentle voice like gliding water's song:
"None from my loins have ever birth
    But they to joy and love belong;
I faithful am, and give to thee
Blessings great—and give them free.

7

"I have woven shrouds of air
In a loom of hurrying light,
For the trees which blossoms bear,
And gilded them with sheets of bright:
I fall upon the grass like love's first kiss,
I make the golden flies and their fine bliss.

"I paint the hedgerows in the lane,
And clover white and red the pathways bear;
I laugh aloud in sudden gusts of rain
To see the Ocean lash himself in air;
I throw smooth shells and weeds along the beach,
And pour the curling waves far o'er the glassy
reach;
Swing birds' nests in the elms, and shake cool moss
Along the aged beams, and hide their loss.

"The very broad rough stones I gladden, too—
Some willing seeds I drop along their sides,
Nourish the generous plant with freshening dew,
Till there where all was waste true joy abides.
The peaks of aged mountains, with my care,
Smile in the red of glowing morn, elate;
I bind the caverns of the sea with hair
Glossy and long, and rich as king's estate;
I polish the green ice, and gleam the wall
With whitening frost, and leaf the brown trees
tall.

SUNDAY POEM

VI

"Thee not alone I leave—far more
  Weave I for thee than for the air;
Thou art of greater worth than the sea-shore,
  And yet for it how much do I prepare!
    I love thee better than the trees—
    Yet I give them sun and breeze;
    More than rivers thou to me,
    More I shall be giving thee;
    Tears of thine I 'll dry fore'er,
    To thee joys and blisses bear.

  "Believe thy Mother for her worth
    (And thou art a son of Earth).
    Thou hadst many years of woe;
    Life was many times thy foe;
    But the stars have looked from where
    Hang their sparklets in the air,
    And their faith is pledged to me
    That they shall give joy to thee."

VII

It came upon me in a sudden thrill,
  It stood before me—'t was a thing of life.
The thoughts rushed out; I had not form nor will;
  I was in hurrying trance, yet felt no strife.

I laughed aloud—Death had crept back awhile;
I looked abroad—the sunlight seemed to smile.
  Joy, joy! was now the song,
  Like a torrent crowding strong
  To the endless Sea along.
She stood before me in that veil of form
 (The stars' first light, dropt from an urn of air);
Within her eyes there melted sunlight warm,
 Which its soft heat did with the moonbeam share;
The gushing of her smile was like a stream
 Which, when all round was crisped with feathery
  snow,
Went surging through the drear its liquid dream,
 In sweet dissolved style, as angels know.
The spell that dwelt within each faintest word
Was Love—the first my eager ear had heard.
  She stood before me, and her life sank through
  My withering heart as doth the piercing dew,
  That sinks with quivering tenderness within
  The moss-rose breast—till it to ope doth win.

VIII

 'T was so—'t was thine! Earth, thou wert true!
  I kneel—thy grateful child, I kneel;
Thy full forgiveness for my sins I sue.
  O Mother! learn thy son can think and feel.
   Mother dear! wilt pardon one
   Who loved not the generous sun,

SUNDAY POEM

Nor thy seasons loved to hear
Chanting to the busy year;
Thee neglected, shut his heart—
In thy being had no part!
Mother! now I list thy song
In this autumn eve along,
As thy chill airs round the day,
Leaving me my time to pray.

Mother dear! the day must come
When thy child shall make his home—
My long, last home—'mid the grass
Over which thy warm hands pass.
Ah me! then do let me lie
Gently on thy breast to die!

I know my prayers will reach thine ear—
Thou art with me while I ask;
Nor thy child refuse to hear,
Who would learn his little task.
Let me take my part with thee
In the gray clouds, or the light—
Laugh with thee upon the sea,
Or idle on the land by night;
In the trees will I with thee—
In the flowers, like any bee.

11

IX

I feel it shall be so ; we were not born
    To sink our finer feelings in the dust ;
Far better to the grave with feelings torn—
    So in our step strides Truth and honest trust
In the great love of things—than to be slaves
    To forms—whose ringing side each stroke we
        give
Stamps with a hollower void ;—yes, to our graves
    Hurrying or e' er we in the heavens' look live
Strangers to our best hopes, and fearing men,
Yea, fearing death—and to be born again.

A SONNET TO JOYCE HETH,
CENTENAKIAN

(1835)

INTOLERABLE Time grasps eagerly,
 With hideous Destiny, who sits him near;
Some name him Fate—it matters not to me,
 So that thy awful durance shall appear.
Old ebon Heth, eternal Black! strange sight!
 Strange, that thou dost not bend to Father Time,
 But, rather, holdest confident thy prime,
In this quick-speeding world, where hovers Night.

Yes, bleached Anatomy! dry skin and bone!
 Thou Grasshopper! thou bloodless, fleshless thing,
 That still, with thin long tongue dost gayly sing!
I would not meet thee at broad noon alone;
 For much I fear thee, and thy yellow fingers,
 Thy cold, sepulchral eye, where moonlight
 lingers.[1]

---

[1] This woman was shown in Boston and elsewhere as the nurse of George
Washington, and about one hundred and sixty years old; she was, in fact,
over one hundred. This sonnet is one of the three earliest poems, the
November Day and *The Spider* preceding it; all were written before Channing was seventeen.

13

THE GIFTS

A DROPPING shower of spray
    Filled with a beam of light;
The breath of smiling Day,
    The groves in wan moonlight;
        Yon river's flow,
        Some falling snow,
    Some bird's swift flight;

A summer field o'erstrewn
    With gay and laughing flowers,
And shepherds' clocks half-blown
    That tell the merry hours;
        The spring's soft rain,
        The waving grain;—
    Are these things *ours?*

LIFE

IT is a gay and glittering cloud
　　Born in the early light of day;
It lies upon the gentle hills,
　　Rosy and sweet and far away.

It burns again when noon is high—
　　Like molten gold it 's clothed in light;
As beautiful and glad as love,
　　A joyous, soul-entrancing sight.

But now it 's fading in the west
　　As helpless as a withered leaf,
As faint as shadow on the grass
　　Thrown by the gleam of moonlight brief.

So Life is born, grows up, and dies,
　　A cloud upon the world of light;
It comes in joy and moves in love,
　　Then gently fades away in night.

THE STARS

SILENT companions of the blinded Earth,
Day's recollection, enemies of Time!
How like an angel troop, with folded hopes
Ye patient stand, each separate in the azure!

Hark to the rushing of the midnight wind
Falling, with his resistless scymitar,
Upon the mournful foliage of the wood!
Whirling before it, to the South they flee,
In sad confusion to the sheltering South;
The yellow grass moans in the chilling air,
Each living thing runs to its indoor home—
But ye, clear Stars, look with untrembling eyes
On the fierce blast—far in your upper sphere.

Where the wild battle rages, till the streams
Run crimson to the sea, and frightened Death
Falls shuddering at the slaughter, pressing hard
His icy palms upon his saddened eyes—
Your mild and dewy light floats gently o'er,
Sweet as a mother's thought of sleeping babes.

Through your deep light I look, and see the abode
Of greater spirits than our life sends forth
In paths of the green earth to wander wide:
I see a wisdom which our noisy day,

16

THE STARS

That jars our phantom forms in rude uproar,
Shall never emulate.   Unsleeping Stars !
Who then distrusts the Love that rules the world,
Or thinks, though unheard, that your sphere is
    dumb?

A POET'S LOVE

THE running winds are not more fleet
That pace along the blue sea's floor
Than were thy tender childhood's feet,
    O Girl, the best that nature bore!

        I can remember well
            In very early youth
        My sumptuous Isabel,
            Who was a girl of truth—
    Of golden truth; we may not often see
    Those whose whole lives have only known—to be.

        The cottage where she dwelt
            Was all o'er mosses green;
        I still forever felt
            How nothing stands between
    The soul and truth; why, starving poverty
    Was nothing—nothing, Isabel, to thee.

        Grass beneath her faint tread
            Bent pleasantly away;
        From her no small birds fled,
            But kept at their bright play,
    Not fearing her—such was her endless motion,
    Just a true swell upon a summer ocean.

18

A POET'S LOVE

They who conveyed her home—
I mean who led her where
The spirit does not roam—
Had such small weight to bear
They scarcely felt it; softly was the knell
Rung for thee that soft day, girl Isabel!

I dwell no more below:
My life is raised on high.
My fantasy was slow
Ere Isabel could die;
It pressed me down; but now I sail away
Into the regions of exceeding day.

There Isabel and I
Float on the red-brown clouds
That amply multiply
The fair inconstant crowds
Of shapes serene.   Play on, Mortality!
Thy happiest hour is that when thou mayst die.

ODE. THE RIVER

THE River calmly flows
   Through shining banks, through lonely
    glen,
Where the owl shrieks, though ne'er the cheer
    of men
Has stirred its mute repose;
Still, if you should walk there, you would go
    there again.

   The stream is well alive;
   Another passive world you see,
   Where downward grows the form of every tree;
    Like soft light clouds they thrive;
Like them, let us in our pure loves reflected be!

   A yellow gleam is thrown
   Into the secrets of that maze
   Of tangled trees, that late shut out our gaze,
    Refusing to be known;
It must its privacy unclose, its glories blaze.

   Sweet falls the summer air
   Over her form who sails with me;
   Her way, like it, is beautifully free,
    Her nature far more rare;
And is her constant heart of virgin purity.

20

ODE. THE RIVER

A quivering star is seen
Keeping its watch above the hill,
Though from the sun's retreat small light is
    still
    Poured on Earth's saddening mien.
We all are tranquilly obeying Evening's will.

Thus ever love the Power!
To simplest thoughts dispose the mind;
In each obscure event a worship find
    Like that of this dim hour,
In lights, and airs, and trees—and in all human-
    kind.

We smoothly glide below
The faintly glimmering worlds of light.
Day has a charm, and this deceptive Night
    Brings a mysterious show;
He shadows our dear Earth--but his cool stars
    are white.

THE EVENING OF A NOVEMBER DAY

THEE, mild autumnal Day,
  I felt not for myself; the winds may steal
From any point, and seem to me alike
  Reviving, soothing powers.

Like thee the contrast is
Of a new mood in a decaying man,
Whose idle mind is suddenly revived
  With many pleasant thoughts.

Our earth was gratified;
Fresh grass, a stranger in this frosty time,
Peeped from the crumbling mould, as welcome as
  An unexpected friend.

How glowed the evening star!
As it delights to glow in summer's midst,
When out of ruddy boughs the twilight birds
  Sing flowing harmony.

22

THE EVENING OF A NOVEMBER DAY

Peace was the will to-day;
Love, in bewildering growth, our joyous minds
Swelled to their widest bounds; the Worldly left
All hearts to sympathize.

I felt for Thee—for Thee,
Whose inward, outward life completely moves,
Surrendered to the beauty of the Soul,
On this creative day.

TO CLIO

PLANETS bear thee in their hands,
  Azure skies fold over thee;
Thou art sung by angel bands
  And the deep, cold-throbbing sea,
  Whispered in each sighing tree
  And each meadow's melody.

Where the sprites outwatch the moon,
  Where the ghostly night-breeze swells,
And the brook prolongs its tune,
  Through the shimmering, shadowed dells,
  To the ringing fairy bells,
  There thou weavest unknown spells.

    In thy folded trance do hide
      Ceaseless measures of content;
    And thou art of Form the bride,
      Shapely Picture's element.

SEA-SONG

WAVES on the beach,—and the wild sea-foam,—
  With a leap and a dash and a sudden cheer,
Where the sea-weed makes its bending home,
  And the sea-birds swim on the crests so clear;
    Wave after wave they are curling o'er,
    And the white sand dazzles along the shore.

Let our boat to the waves go free,
  By the bending tide where the curled wave
    breaks!
  'T is the track of the wind on the white snow-
    flakes.
Away! away! in our path o'er the sea.

Blasts may rave—yet we spread the sail,
  For our spirits can wrest the power from the
    wind,
  And the gray clouds yield to the sunny mind;
Fear not we the whirl of the gale!

THE HARBOR

NO more I seek—the prize is found;
  I furl my sails, the voyage is o'er;
The treacherous waves no longer sound,
  But sing thy praise along the shore.

I did not dream to welcome thee;
  Like all I have, thou cam'st unknown;
An island in a misty sea,
  With stars and flowers and harvests strown.

I steal from all I hoped of old,
  To throw more beauty round thy way;
The dross I part, and melt the gold,
  And stamp it with thy every-day.

A well is in the desert sand,
  With purest water, cold and clear,
Where overjoyed at rest I stand,
  And drink the sound I hoped to hear.

THE BENIGHTED TRAVELLER

THE treacherous dark has razed his homeward
    path;
He journeys on, slow moving o'er the moor,
And, like a spirit from the heavens sent,
Dances before him his old kitchen hearth,
His children round, and antique serving-maid.
The pale stars glimmer through a flickering mist,
While chill the night-breeze creeps about his heart.

His unfamiliar step crushes the herb
That withered long ago, untouched before;
He stumbles o'er rude stones, and climbs the hill
To see the waning moon with pity look
On marshes spread beneath, and endless glades,
Where never fell his eye until this hour.

PICTURES

I. STILL WATER

THOU, lazy river, flowing neither way,
  Me figurest, and yet thy banks seem gay;
I flow between the shores of this large life,
My banks as fair as thine, with joy as rife;
Thy tides will swell when the next moon comes
    round,
But mine far higher in their rise be found.

II. MOONLIGHT

HE came, and waved a little silver wand;
  He dropt the veil that hid a statue fair;
He drew a circle with that pearly hand,
  His grace confined that beauty in the air;
Those limbs so gentle, now at rest from flight,
Those quiet eyes, now musing on the night.

III. CHARACTERS

A GENTLE eye with a spell of its own,
  A meaning glance and a sudden thrill;
A voice—sweet music in every tone;
  A steadfast heart and a resolute will;

28

PICTURES

A graceful form and a cheering smile,
   Ever the same, and always true.
I have heard of this for a long, long while—
   I have seen it, known it, loved it too.

IV. THE CONTRAST

THE gray clouds fly,—
There is war on high,—
Their pennons flying, their soldiers dying;
   They fall in rain,
   But they leave no stain.

But the heart's flight
In the gloomy night,
Its trusting over, its changing lover!
   There falls no rain,
   But tears that pain.

WILLINGNESS

AN unendeavoring flower—how still
   Its growth from morn to even-time !
No signs of haste or anger fill
   Its tender form, from birth to prime
     Of happy will.

And some, who think these simple things
   Can bear no lesson to our minds,
May learn to feel what Nature brings,
   And round a quiet being winds,
     And through us sings.

A stream to some is no delight,
   Its elements diffused around ;
Yet in its unobtrusive flight
   There trembles from its wave a sound
     Like that of Night.

Take then thine own allotment fair,
   To others turn a social heart ;
And if thy days pass clear as air,
   Or friends from thy beseeching part,
     Both humbly bear !

AMONG THE LENOX HILLS

DEAR Friend! in this fair atmosphere again,
Far from the noisy echoes of the main,
Amid the world-old mountains, and these hills,
From whose strange grouping a fine power distils
A soothing and a calm, I seek repose,
The city's noise forgot—its hard, stern woes.

As thou once saidst, the rarest sons of earth
Have in the dust of cities shown their worth,
Where long collision with the human curse
Has of great glory been the frequent nurse;
And only those who in sad cities dwell
Are of the green trees fully sensible;
To them the silver bells of tinkling streams
Seem brighter than an angel's laugh in dreams.

Here dawn, full noon, evening, and solemn night
Weave all around their robes of changing light;
And in the mighty forest Day's whole time
Is shadowed with a portraiture sublime:
In the dark caves dwells Midnight in her stole,
While shady Even haunts a tranquil knoll.

COMPANIONSHIP

MY mind obeys the Power
    That through all persons breathes;
The woods are murmuring,
And fields begin to sing,
    And in me Nature wreathes.

Thou too art with me here,
    The best of all design;
Of that strong purity
Which makes it joy to be
    A distant thought of thine.

THE SEASONS

I. SPRING

LEAVES on the trees,
 And buds in the breeze,
And tall grass waves on the meadow's side ;
 And a showerlet sweet,
 While the light clouds meet
In their golden robes, when Day has died.

The Scholar his pen
 Hath mended again,
For the new life runs in his wearied veins ;
 And the glad child flies
 To the flowers' fresh dyes,
And the happy bird gushes with sudden strains.

II. AUTUMN'S APPROACH

SUMMER is going,
 Cold wind is blowing—
Sign of the autumn, the autumn so drear ;
 No sower is sowing,
 No mower is mowing—
Seed is sown, harvest mown, Time 's almost sere.

33

Flowers are fading,
Autumn's wreath 's braiding,
To deck the sad burial, burial so lone;
Bees have done lading,
Finished their trading—
Honey made, cellars laid, hive almost grown.

Gray clouds are flying,
Gray shades replying;
Soon shall come mourning—mourning and wail;
The babe shall be crying,
The mother be sighing.
Coldly lie, coldly die, in the arms of thy gale!

III. WINTER

COLD blows the blast,
And the snow falls fast
On meadow and moor and the deep blue lakes;
In the snow-white sheen
The wind is as keen
As the glances which Envy makes.

Merrily by the hearthstone we
Sit with a song of social glee,
While the blaze of the red fire glows,
Painting the sides of the rafters old
Till they shine in the roof like melted gold,
Under the piled-up, chilling snows.

34

THE SEASONS

Now the brooks are bound,
They make no sound,
Still as the corpse in its coffin drear;
While the icicles shine
As stately and fine
As the lamps of the church o'er the death-cold
bier.

Winter troubleth not thus;
There are joys for us:
Thine eye is as warm as in summer-time,
Thy kiss is as sweet,
And thy loving arms meet
As when rang abroad the soft wind's chime.

THE SIBYL TO HER LOVER

ROAM—the wide world before thee—
  O'er mount and vale, o'er stream and sea!
Roam! outspread before the gale,
Even if it rend, thy swelling sail!
  Beware of the sunny isles!
  Trust not their rosy smiles!

I—what am I to thee!
A speck on thy morning sea;
Soon shalt thou forget me,
Thou honey-gathering bee!
With thy laden freight shalt pass
  Over all the earth to-day,
Sweeping o'er the bending grass
  Beneath the wild air's play.

Set thy canvas to the wind,
  Thy rudder man for ocean war!
Speeding, leave the land behind,
  Thy rushing course pursuing far!
    Beware of the sunny isles!
    Trust not their rosy smiles!

36

THE SIBYL TO HER LOVER

Look not on Beauty for thy mate,
  Nor sparkling wine, nor fantasy!
But drink the perfect desolate
  Of some wild, lofty misery,
    With nervèd hand, and sparkling free!
    Beware of the sunny isles!
    Trust not their rosy smiles!

Bide not thy time, heed not thy fate!
  Believe no truth, respect no law!
Fling to the winds old Custom's state,
  And play with every antique saw!
    And warm and sweet thy life shall be,
    Across the fathoms of the sea.

Wait but the hour—thy course is run;
  Life's carpentry will build no more;
Thou shalt sit silenced in the dun
  Perpetual tempest's sluggish roar;
    Those velvet tresses then shall be
    Slimed and disfigured in the sea.

Away! away! thou starlit breath!
  On bended knees I pray thee, go!
Oh, bind thy temples not with death,
  Nor let thy shadow fall on snow!

37

Spread thy broad canvas to the breeze,
Thy bows surrender to the seas!
Beware of the sunny isles!
Trust not their rosy smiles!

Thy music shall the sunset-star
Tune spherally in liquid light;
Thy jewelled couch the South inbar
Within the curtains of her night,
And fold thee in her clustering arms,
To sing thee deep in dreamiest charms.

OCTOBER

DRY leaves, with yellow ferns, they are
   Fit wreath of autumn—while a star
 Still, bright, and pure our frosty air
   Shivers in twinkling points
   Of thin, celestial hair;
 And thus one side of Heaven anoints.

Most quiet in this sheltered nook
Am I, beneath the moon's calm look,
   From trouble of the frosty wind
   That curls the yellow blade:
   Though in my covert mind
 A grateful sense of change is made.

To wandering men how dear this sight
Of a cold, tranquil autumn night,
   In its majestic, deep repose!
   Thus should their genius be,
   Not buried in high snows,
 Though of as mute tranquillity.

An anxious life they will not pass,
Nor, as the shadow on the grass,

Leave no impression there to stay;
To them all things are thought;
The blushing Morn's decay,
Our death, our life, by this is taught.

Oh, find in every haze that shines
A brief appearance without lines,
A single word—no finite joy;
For present is a Power
Which we may not annoy,
Yet love him stronger every hour.

I would not put this sense from me
If I could some great sovereign be;
Yet will not task a fellow-man
To feel the same glad sense;
For no one living can
Feel, save his given influence.

UNA

TO ELIZABETH HOAR

WE are centred deeper far
  Than the eye of any star,
Nor can rays of long sunlight
Thread a pace of our delight.

In thy form I see the day
  Burning, of a kingdom higher,
In thy silver network play
  Thoughts that to the Gods aspire;
In thy cheek I see the flame
  Of thy studious taper burn;
And thy Grecian eye might tame
  Natures ashed in antique urn.

So trembling meek, so proudly strong,
Thou dost to higher worlds belong
Than where I sing this empty song:
Yet I, a thing of mortal kind,
Can kneel before thy pathless mind,
And see in thee what my mates say
Sank o'er Judea's hills one crimson day.

Yet flames on high the keen Greek fire,
  And later ages rarefies,
And even on my tuneless lyre
  A faint, wan beam of radiance dies.

And might I say what I have thought
  Of thee and those I love to-day,
Then had the world an echo caught
  Of that intense, impassioned lay,
Which sung in those thy being sings,
And from the deepest ages rings.

THE POOR

I DO not mourn my friends are false—
    I dare not grieve for sins of mine;
I weep for those who pine to death,
    Great God! in this rich world of thine.
These by their darkened hearthstones sit,
    Their children shivering idly round;
As true as living God, 't were fit
    For these poor men to curse the ground!

And those who daily bread have none,—
    Half starved the long, long winter's day,—
Fond parents gazing on their young,
    Too wholly sad one word to say:
To them it seems their God has cursed
    This race of ours since they were born;
Willing to toil—and yet deprived
    Of common wood, or store of corn.

I do not weep for mine own woes;
    They are as nothing in my eye.
I weep for them who, starved and froze,
    Do curse their God and long to die.

NATURE

BLUE is the sky as ever, and the stars
   Kindle their crystal flames at soft-fallen Eve
With the same purest lustre that the East
Worshipt; the river gently flows through fields
Wherein the broad-leaved corn spreads out and
     loads
Its ear, as when its Indian tilled the soil;
The dark green pine, green in the winter's cold,
Still whispers meaning emblems as of old;
The cricket chirps, and the sweet, eager birds
In the sad woods crowd their thick melodies;
But yet, to common eyes, life's poesy
Something has faded.

THE SEA

SOUND on, thou anthem of the breathless Soul,
  Unneeding heat, unfathomed and alone!
Thy waves in measured phalanx firmly roll,
  And meet the furious wind in steadfast tone.

Sweet smiles the day-god on thy green expanse,
  And purples thee with his sad, fading eve;
Yet all the livelong night thy waters dance,
  As mariners the favoring harbors leave.

Thy sunken rocks are nigh the inconstant shore;
  There thou hast tribute from the fisher's boat.
Afar thou art the play of him no more,
  But mighty ships on thy high mountains float.

DEATH

BENEATH the endless surges of the deep,
  Whose green content o'erlaps them evermore,
A host of mariners perpetual sleep,
  Too hushed to heed the wild commotion's roar;
The emerald weeds glide softly o'er their bones,
And wash them gently 'mid the rounded stones.

No epitaph have they to tell their tale;
  Their birthplace, age, and story all are lost;
Yet rest they deeply as, within this vale,
  These sheltered bodies by the smooth slates crost;
And countless tribes of men lie on the hills,
And human blood runs in the crystal rills.

The air is full of men who once enjoyed
  The healthy element, nor looked beyond;
Many who all their mortal strength employed
  In human kindness, of their brothers fond;
And many more who counteracted fate,
And battled in the strife of common hate.

Profoundest sleep enwraps them all around—
  Sages and sires, the child and manhood strong:
Shed not one tear, expend no sorrowing sound!
  Tune thy clear voice to no funereal song!

46

DEATH

For Death stands there to welcome thee and me,
And Life hath yet a steeper mystery.

O Death! thou art the palace of our hopes,
    The storehouse of our joys, great labor's end;
Thou art the bronzed key which swiftly opes
    The coffers of the Past; and thou shalt send
Such trophies to our hearts as sunny days,
When Life upon its golden harpstrings plays.

And when a nation mourns a silent voice
    That long entranced its ear with melody,
How must thou in thy inmost soul rejoice
    To wrap such treasures in thy boundless sea!
And thou wert dignified if but one soul
Had been enfolded in thy twilight stole.

Triumphal arches circle o'er thy deep,
    Dazzling with jewels, radiant with content;
In thy vast arms the sons of genius sleep—
    The carvings of their spheral monument
Bearing no recollection of dim Time
Within thy green and most perennial prime.

Thou art not anxious of thy precious fame,
    But comest like the clouds, soft stealing on;
Thou soundest in a careless key his name
    Who to thy boundless treasury is won;
And yet he quickly cometh; for to die
Is ever gentlest, both to low and high.

Thou therefore hast Humanity's respect;
   They build thee tombs along the green hillside,
And will not suffer thee the least neglect,
   But tend thee with a desolate, sad pride:
For thou art strong, O Death! though sweetly so,
And in thy lovely gentleness sleeps woe.

I come—I come! think not I turn away!
   Fold round me thy gray robe! I stand to feel
The setting of my last frail, earthly day:
   I will not pluck it off, but calmly kneel.
For I am great as thou art,—though not thou,—
And Thought, as with thee, dwells upon my brow.

Ah! might I ask thee, Spirit, first to tend
   Upon those dear ones whom my heart has found?
And supplicate thee that I might them lend
   A light in their last hours, and to the ground
Consign them still? Yet think me not too weak—
Come to me now, and thou shalt find me meek.

Then let us live in fellowship with thee;
   Turn ruddy cheeks unto thy kisses pale,
And listen to thy song as minstrelsy,
   And still revere thee, till our heart-throbs fail:
Sinking within thine arms as sinks the sun
Below the farthest hills when his day's work is done.

SONNETS OF LOVE AND ASPIRATION

I

THOU art like that which is most sweet and
    fair,
  A gentle morning in the youth of Spring,
  When the few early birds begin to sing
Within the delicate depths of the fine air;
Yet shouldst thou these dear beauties much impair,
  Since thou art better than is everything
  Which either woods or skies or green fields bring;
And finer thoughts hast thou than they can wear.

In the proud sweetness of thy grace I see
  What lies within—a pure and steadfast mind,
Which its own mistress is of sanctity,
  And to all gentleness hath been refined;
So that thy least breath falleth upon me
  As the soft breathing of midsummer wind.

II [1]

The Summer's breath, that laughed among the
    flowers,
  Caressed the tender blades of the soft grass,
  And o'er thy dear form with its joy did pass,
Has left us now. These are but Autumn-hours,

[1] Addressed to Ellen Fuller (1841), as I think the first sonnet was.

And in their melancholy vestures glass
A feeling that belongs to deeper powers
Than haunt the warm-eyed June or spring-time
    showers—
The destiny of them like us, alas!

Think not of Time; there is a better sphere
    Rising above these cold and shadowy days—
A softer music than the gray clouds hear,
    That spread their flying sails above our ways,
Where rustle in the breeze the thin leaves sere,
    Or on the leaden air dance in swift maze.

III

I mark beneath thy life the virtue shine
    That deep within the star's eye opes its day;
    I clutch the gorgeous thoughts thou throw'st
    away
From thy profound, unfathomable mine,
And with them this mean, common hour do twine,
    As glassy waters o'er the dry beach play;
And I were rich as Night them to combine
    With my poor store, and warm me in thy ray.

SONNETS OF LOVE

From the fixed answer of those dateless eyes
    I meet bold hints of Spirit's mystery
As to what 's past—and hungry prophecies
    Of deeds to-day, and things which are to be;
Of lofty life that with the eagle flies,
    And lowly love, that clasps humanity.

IV

Earth hath her meadows green, her brooklets
    bright;
    She hath a myriad flowers that bloom aloft—
    O ershades her peerless glances with clouds soft,
And on her sward dances the capering light;
She hath a full glad day, a solemn night,
    And showers, and trees, and waterfallings oft.
I am as one who ministers her rite—
Meekly I love her, and in her delight:

But so much soul hast thou within thy form,
    Than luscious summer days thou art yet more;
And far within thee there is that more warm
    Than ever sunlight to the wild flowers bore—
Thou who art mine to love and to revere,
Thou great glad gentleness, and sweetly clear!

V

Hearts of Eternity! hearts of the deep!
   Proclaim from land to sea your mighty fate—
   How that for you no living comes too late,
How ye cannot in Theban labyrinth creep,
How ye great harvest from small surface reap;
   Shout, excellent Band, in grand primeval strain,
   Like midnight winds that foam along the main!
And do all things rather than pause to weep.

A human heart knows naught of littleness,
   Suspects no man, compares with no one's ways—
   Hath in one hour most glorious length of days,
A recompense, a joy, a loveliness:
   Like eagle keen, shoots into azure far,
   And, always dwelling nigh, is the remotest star.

VI

I love the universe—I love the joy
   Of every living thing. Be mine the sure
   Felicity which ever shall endure!
While Passion whirls its madmen, as they toy,
To hate, I would my simple life employ
   In the calm-pouring sunlight—in that pure
   And motionless silence ever would assure
My best true powers, without a thought's annoy.

See, and be glad! O high imperial race!
Dwarfing the common altitude of strength,—
Learn that ye stand on an unshaken base!
  Be glad in woods, o'er sands, by marsh or
    streams!
Your powers will carry you to any length.
  Up! earnestly feel these gentle sunset beams!

THE SLEEPING CHILD

(WALDO EMERSON, DEAD)
(1843)

DARKNESS now hath overpaced
Life's swift dance; and curtained Awe
Feebly lifts a sunken eye,
Wonted to this gloomy law.
Lips are still that sweetly spoke;
Heedless Death the spell hath broke.

Weep not for him, friends so dear!
Largest measure he hath taken.
Now he roams the sun's dominion,
Our chill fortunes quite forsaken;
There his eyes have purer sight
In that calm, reflected light.

Let your tears dissolve in peace!
For he holds high company;
And he seeks, with famous men,
Statelier lines of ancestry;
He shall shame the wisest ones
In that palace of the suns.

ENGLAND, IN AFFLICTION

(1843)

THOU Sea of circumstance, whose waves are ages,
  On whose high surf the fates of men are
    thrown!
Thou writing from the calm, eternal pages,
  Whose letters secret unto Him alone
  Who writ that scroll forever shall be known!
I deem not of thy inmost to discover,
Yet oh, forget not I am thy true lover.

Home of the Brave! deep-centred in the Ocean—
  Cradle where rocked the famous bards of old,
Consummate masters of the heart's emotion,
  Free, genial intellects by Heaven made bold!
  My blood I should disown, and deem me cold,
If I did not revere thy matchless sons—
Of all Time's progeny the noblest ones.

What though the calm Elysium of the air
  Hangs violet draperies o'er the Grecian fanes?
What though the fields of Italy are fair?
  Above them England towers, with mightier
    gains;
  Yet, tell me, are her sons bound fast in chains?

The fearful note of misery sounds so high
From her wide plains up to her clouded sky.

In woodland churches rising forest-free,
   Network of threaded granite, textured fine,
And stamped with countenance of sanctity,—
   With arches waving like the pointed pine,
   Where spires and cones and rugged barks
      entwine,—
Their cloisters shadowy in the light of noon,
Their tall, dim steeples misty in the moon;

Thy surplice—shall it hide a purse of gold?
   The smooth and roted sermon doff to Fame?
Extinguished every aspiration bold,
   While only sounds some formal, empty name?
   Shall her old churches make proud England
      tame?
Throw ashes in those hearts where once coursed
      blood,
And blind those streaming eyes from sight of
      good?

England!—the name hath bulwarks in the sound,
   And bids her people own the State again;
Bids them to dispossess their native ground
   From out the hands of titled noblemen;
   Then shall the scholar freely wield his pen,

56

ENGLAND, IN AFFLICTION

And shepherds dwell where lords keep castle
   now,
And peasants cut the overhanging bough.

Fold not thy brawny arms as though thy toil
   Was done, nor take thy drowsy path toward
   sleep!
There never will be leisure on thy soil,
   There never will be idless on thy steep;
   So long as thou sailst the unsounded deep,
New conquests shall be thine, new heritage,
Such as the world's whole wonder must engage.

THE BEGGAR'S WISH

(1843)

O SPARE from all thy luxury
   A tear for one who may not weep!
Whose heart is like a wintry sea,
   So still and cold and deep.

Nor shed that tear till I am laid
   Beneath the fresh-dug turf at rest,
And o'er my grave the elm-tree's shade
   That hides the robin's nest.

A POET'S HOPE

The tradition of the composition of this daring poem is thus: Ellery Channing, a young poet, was calling on the wife of his friend S. G. Ward, herself a vision of grace and beauty — "tremulous with grace," said Emerson. She challenged him, in conversation half serious, to write her a poem; he withdrew into an anteroom where were writing-materials, and, offhand, in a very short time had improvised these verses, now the best known, by reason of their last line, of all his early poems. It would be hard to match the whole piece for wild and sustained imagination and a magical harmony of verse in its best stanzas.

FLYING—flying beyond all lower regions,
　Beyond the light called Day, and Night's
　　repose,
Where the untrammelled soul, on her wind-pinions
　Fearlessly sweeping, defies my earthly woes;
There, there, upon that infinitest sea,
Lady! thy hope—so fair a hope—summons me.

Fall off, ye garments of my misty weather!
　Drop from my eyes, ye scales of Time's applying!
Am I not godlike? Meet not here together
　A Past and Future infinite, defying
The cold, still, callous moment of To-day?
Am I not master of the calm alway?

Unloose me, demons of dull Care and Want!
　I will not stand your slave—I am your king:
Think not within your meshes vile I pant
　For the wild liberty of an unclipped wing!
My empire is myself, and I defy
The external; yes, I rule the whole, or die!

All music that the fullest breeze can play
 In its melodious whisperings in the wood,
All modulations which entrance the day
 And deify a sunlight solitude,
All anthems that the waves sing to the Ocean
Are mine for song—and yield to my devotion.

Lady! there is a hope that all men have—
 Some mercy for their faults, a grassy place
To rest in, and a flower-strown gentle grave;
 Another hope doth purify our race—
That when the fearful bourne 's forever past,
They may find rest—and rest *so* long to last!

I seek it not; I ask no rest forever;
 My path is onward to the farthest shores:
Upbear me in your arms, unceasing River,
 That from the Soul's clear fountain swiftly pours!
Motionless not, until that end is won
Which now I feel hath scarcely felt the sun.

To feel, to know—to soar unlimited
 'Mid throngs of light-winged angels sweeping
 far,
And pore upon the realms unvisited
 That tessellate some unseen, unthought Star!
To be the thing that now I feebly dream,
Flashing within my faintest, deepest gleam.

A POET'S HOPE

Ah, caverns of my soul! how thick your shade,
  Where glows that light by which I faintly see!
Wave your bright torches! for I need your aid,
  Golden-eyed demons of my ancestry!
Your son, now blinded, hath a light within,
A heavenly fire—which ye from suns did win.

O Time! O Death! I clasp you in my arms;
  For I can soothe an infinite cold sorrow,
Gazing contented on your icy charms,
  And that wild snow-pile which we call To-
    morrow:
Sweep o'er, O soft and azure-lidded sky!
Earth's waters to your genial gaze reply.

I am not earth-born, though I here delay;
  Hope's child, I summon infiniter powers,
And laugh to see the mild and sunny day
  Smile on the shrunk and thin autumnal hours.
I laugh, for Hope hath happy place with me:
If my bark sinks, 't is to another sea.

POEMS OF YOUTHFUL
FAMILY LIFE

Taken chiefly from the edition of 1847

NEW ENGLAND

I WILL not sing for gain, nor yet for fame,
  Though praise I shall enjoy if come it may;
I will not sing to make my nature tame—
  And thus it is if I seek Fortune's way:
  But I will chant a rude heroic lay
On rough New England's coast, whose sterile soil
Gives happiness and dignity to Toil.

In a New England hand the lyre must beat
  With brave emotions; such the winter wind
Sweeps on chill pinions, when the cutting sleet
  Doth the bare traveller in the fields half blind,
  And, freezing to the trees, congeals a rind
Next day more brilliant than the Arab skies,
Or plumes from gorgeous birds of paradise.

A bold and nervous hand must strike the strings—
  Our varying climate forms its children so;
And what we lack in Oriental things
  We render good by that perpetual blow
  Which wears away the strongest rocks, we
    know;
Sure in supply, and constant in demand—
Active and patient—fit to serve or stand.

They do malign us who contract our hope
  To prudent gain or blind religious zeal;
More signs than these shine in our horoscope—
  Nobly to live, to do, and dare, and feel,
  Knit to each other by firm bands of steel;
Our eyes to God we turn, our hearts to Home,
Standing content beneath the azure dome.

My Country! 't is for thee I strike the lyre;
  My Country, wide as is the free wind's flight!
I sing New England, as she lights her fire
  In every Prairie's midst, and where the bright
  Enchanting stars shine pure through Southern
    night;
She still is there, a guardian on the tower,
To open for the world a purer hour.

Could they but know the wild, enchanting thrill
  That in our homely houses fills the heart!
Or feel how faithfully New England's will
  Beats in each artery and each small part
  Of this great Continent, their blood would start
In Georgia, or where Spain once sat in state,
Or Texas, 'neath her lone star desolate.

NEW ENGLAND

Because they shall be free,—we wish it thus;
  In vain against our purpose may they turn!
They are our brothers and belong to us—
  And on our altars Slavery shall burn,
  Its ashes buried in a silent urn.
Think not this is a vain New England boast!
We love the distant West, the Atlantic coast.

'T is our New England thought to make this land
  The very home of Freedom, the sure nurse
Of each sublime emotion; she doth stand
  Between the sunny South and the dread curse
  Of God—who else should her whole race
    inhearse,
With condemnation to this Union's life:
We stand to heal this plague, and banish strife.[1]

I do not sing of this, but hymn the day
  That gilds our cheerful villages and plains,
Our hamlets, strewn at distance on each way,
  Our forests, and our ancient streams' domains;
  We are a band of brothers, and our gains
Are freely shared; no beggar in our roads,
Content and peace within our fair abodes.

---

[1] It should be remembered that this was written nearly twenty
years before final emancipation.

In my small cottage on the lonely hill,[1]
   Where like a hermit I must bide my time,
Surrounded by a landscape lying still
   All seasons through, as in this winter's prime,—
   Rude, and as homely as these verses chime,—
I have a satisfaction which no king
Has often felt—if Fortune's happiest thing.

'T is not my fortune—which is mainly low;
   'T is not my merit—that is nothing worth;
'T is not that I have stores of Thought below,
   Which everywhere might build up Heaven on
      earth;
   Nor was I highly favored in my birth;
Few friends have I—and they are much to me,
Yet fly above my poor society.[2]

But all about me live New England men,—
   Their humble houses meet my daily gaze,—
The children of this land, where life again
   Flows like a great stream in sunshiny ways;
   This is my joy,—to know them,—and my days
Are filled with love to meditate on them—
These native gentlemen on Nature's hem.

---

[1] Ponkatasset.
[2] These, in 1840, were Alcott, Emerson, Hawthorne, and Thoreau.

NEW ENGLAND

If I could take one feature of their life,
  Then on my page a mellow light should shine:
Their days are holy days, with labor rife—
  Labor, the song of praise, that sounds divine,
  And better than all sacred hymns of mine;
The patient Earth sets platters for their food—
Corn, milk, and apples, and the best of good.

See here no shining scenes for artist's eye—
  This woollen frock shall make no painter's fame,
These homely tools all burnishing defy;
  The beasts are slow and heavy, still or tame;
  The sensual eye may think this labor lame;
T is in the Man where lies the sweetest art,
And his endeavor in his earnest part.

The wind may blow a hurricane, but he
  Goes fairly onward with the thing in hand;
He sails undaunted on the crashing sea,
  Beneath the keenest winter frost doth stand;
  And by his will he makes his way command—
Till every season smiles delight to feel
The grasp of his hard hand, encased in steel.

He meets the year confiding; no great throws
  That suddenly bring riches doth he use;
But like Thor's hammer vast, his patient blows
  Vanquish his difficult tasks; he doth refuse
  To tread the path, nor know the way he views:

No sad, complaining words he uttereth,
But draws in peace a free and hearty breath.

I love to meet him on the frozen road;
  How manly is his eye, as clear as air!
He cheers his beasts without the brutal goad;
  His face is ruddy and his features fair,
  His brave "Good day" sounds like an honest
    prayer.
This man is in his place; he feels his trust;
'T is not dull plodding through the heavy crust.

And when I have him at his pleasant hearth,
  Within his homestead, where no ornament
Glows on his mantel but his own true worth,
  I feel as if within an Arab's tent;
  His hospitality is more than meant;
I there am welcome as the sunlight is—
I must feel warm to be a friend of his.

This man takes pleasure o'er the crackling fire;
  His glittering axe subdued the monarch oak—
He earned the cheerful blaze by something higher
  Than pensioned blows; he owned the tree he
    stroke,
  And knows the value of the distant smoke,
When he returns at night, his labor done,
Matched in his action with the long day's sun.

NEW ENGLAND

How many brave adventures with the cold
    Built up this cumbrous cellar of plain stone!
How many summer heats the bricks did mould
    That make this ample fireplace! and the tone
Of twice a thousand winds sings through the zone
Of rustic paling round this modest yard;
These are the verses of this simple bard.

Who sings the praise of Woman in our clime?
    I do not boast her beauty or her grace;
Some humble duties render her sublime—
    She, the sweet nurse of this New England race,
    The flower upon the country's sterile face—
The Mother of New England's sons, the pride
Of every house where those good sons abide.

From early morn to fading eve she stands,
    Labor's best offering on the shrine of worth
(And Labor's jewels glitter on her hands),
    To animate the heaviness of earth,
    To make a plenty out of partial dearth,
To cheer and serve serenely through her pain,
And nurse a vigorous race, and ne'er complain.

There is a Roman splendor in her smile,
    A tenderness that owes its depth to toil;
Well may she leave the smooth, voluptuous wile
    That forms the woman of a softer soil;
    Herself she does pour forth a fragrant oil

Upon the dark asperities of Fate,
And makes a garden—else all desolate.

With natural, honest bearing of their lot,
  Cheerful at work, and happy when 't is done,
They shine like stars within the humblest cot;
  All speak for Freedom, centred all in one;
  From every river's side I hear the son
Of some New England woman answer me:
"Joy to our mothers, who did make us free!"

I never knew New England wife cast down,
  Though terrible indeed have come the blows
Of agony; yet through the storm the crown
  Of gentlest patience rested on her brows;
  Chaste as an icicle,—her marriage vows
Serenely kept,—heroic to the end,
She was the child and mother, wife and friend.

These are our men and women—this the sight
  That greets me daily when I pass their homes;
It is enough for me;—it sheds a light
  Over the gloomiest hours: my fancy roams
  No more to Greece or Italy—the loams
Whereon we tread are sacred by the lives
Of those who till them; and our comfort thrives.

NEW ENGLAND

Vainly ye pine-woods rising on the height
  Should lift your verdant boughs and cones aloft!
Vainly ye winds should surge around in might,
  Or o'er the meadows murmur stanzas soft!
  To me should nothing yield or lake or croft
Had not the figures of the pleasant scene,
Like trees and fields, an innocent demean.

Therefore I love a cold and flinty realm;
  I love the sky that hangs New England o'er;
And if I were embarked, and at the helm,
  I 'd run my vessel on New England's shore,
  And, dashed upon her crags, would live no
    more,
Rather than go to seek a land of graves
Where men who tread the fields are cowering
    slaves.

I love the mossy rocks, so strangely rude,
  The little forests, underwoods and all;
I love the damp paths of the solitude,
  Where, in the tiny brook, some waterfall
  Gives its small shower of diamonds to the thrall
Of light's pursuing reflex, while the trill
Of the cascade enhances silence still.

I love the cold, sad Winter's lengthening while,
  When man doth ache with frost, and Nature
    seems
To leer and grimace with an icy smile—
  And all her little life is held in dreams;
  I love it—even when the far sunbeams
Look through the cloud in faces filled with woe,
Like mourners who to funerals do go.

Search me, ye wintry winds! for I am proof;
  New England's kindness circles through my
    heart.
I see afar that old declining roof,
  Where underneath dwells something that is part
  Of Nature's sweetest music; through me dart
Your coldest spasms! there burns manhood's fire;
I sit by that as warm as I desire.

Or if the torrid August sun scalds down,
  And on my brow stand the big drops like rain,
I can enjoy such fire, and call it crown
  To my content; it ripens golden grain,
  New England corn—I prize the fervid pain;
Some honest hand has planted comfort there,
And fragrant coolness soon steals through the air.

NEW ENGLAND

It is a happy thought that I was born
  In rough New England—here that I may be
Among a race who all mankind adorn,
  A plain, strong race, deep-rooted as a tree.
  And I am most content my ancestry
Dates back no further than New England's date—
What worth hath king or lord where Man is State!

THE WANDERER

"WHO is that wight who wanders there
    So often o'er these lonely fields?
Can solitude his thought repair,
    Or filch the honey that it yields?
I see him often by the Brook;
    He pauses on some little rock,
Or, sheltered in a sunny nook,
    He sits, nor feels the sharp wind's shock.

"I meet him in the lonely lane
    Where merrily I drive my team;
I seek his downcast eye in vain,
    To break the silence of his dream.
Yet sometimes, when I fell the trees,
    He muses with a saddened eye,
While leaps the forest like the seas
    When tide and wind are running high.

"And never questions he a word
    Of what I do or where I go;
His gentle voice I never heard—
    His voice, they say, is sweetly low.
And once, at sunset, on the hill
    He stood, and gazed at scenes afar:
While fell the twilight o'er the rill,
    And glittered in the west a star.

THE WANDERER

"I cannot see his years improve;
  He leaves no tokens on the way;
'T is simply breathing—or to move
  Like some dim spectre through the day;
And yet I love him—for his form
  Is graceful as a maiden's sigh;
And something beautiful and warm
  Is shadowed in his quiet eye."

Thus spoke the driver of the wain
  As solemnly he passed along,
This man, unknown to fame or gain,
  But hero of one Poet's song:
And there he wanders yet, I trust—
  A figure pensive as the scene,
Created from the common dust,
  Yet treading o'er the grasses green.

THE CONCORD SEXTON'S STORY

This story arrested the attention of Hawthorne, then living at the Old
Manse, and he desired to know whence I had obtained it. It is abso-
lutely my sole invention, from beginning to end.—W. E. C. in 1897.

THESE quiet meadows, and the sloping bank
With its green hem of hardy pines, whose
    leaves
The sudden frosts and sodden Autumn rains
Cannot displace, have been the scene of conflict.
Housed in the yielding sand that shapes the bank,
The early Settlers lodged their sturdy frames;
And on these meadows, where the Brook o'erflows,
They saw the Indians glide—their dusky hue
Agreeing with the brown and withered grass:
Their memory yet endures, to paint this scene,
And oft, as I sit musing, they become
Scarcely less living than in days of old.

Noble adventurers! godlike Puritans!
Poets in deed! who came and saw and braved
The accumulated Wilderness, and read therein
The fatal policy of Indian guile—
May we, your sons, thus conquer the wild foes
Who aim their shafts at your sublime design![1]

[1] Alluding, doubtless, to the slave-oligarchy then (in 1846)
annexing Texas and fighting Mexico.

THE CONCORD SEXTON'S STORY

It was a Winter's day. The air came keen
Across the meadows, sheeted with pure snow
New fallen, that now, as downward wheeled the
    day,
Had ceased to fall ; and, the clouds parting off,
Mild showers of light spread o'er the groves and
    fields ;
Then, as the light grew brighter, the wind failed,
And with the calm came a most perfect frost.

The Sexton of our village was an old
And weather-beaten artisan, whose life
Led him to battle with the depths of cold.
Amid the woods he plied a vigorous arm ;
The tall trees crashed in thunder at his stroke,
And a hale cheer was spread about his form.
Death does not stand or falter at the cold,
And our brave Sexton plied his pickaxe bright,
Whether the soft snow fell, or 'mid the rains ;
This day, this Winter's day, he 'd made a grave
For a young blossom that the frost had nipped ;
And, toward the sunset hour, he took his way
Across the meadows wide, and o'er the Brook
Beyond the bridge, and through the leafless arch
Of willows that supports the sunken road,
To the sad house of Death.[1]

---

[1] This describes exactly the turnpike on which, near Emerson's garden,
the poet was, in 1844, living, in the Red Lodge.

The Sexton had forgotten what Death is,
For Death provided him with home and bread,
And graves he dealt in as some deal in farms.
He reached the house of Death,—a friendly
    house,—
And sat in peace to see the wood-fire flash
Its cheerful warmth, and then he spoke as one
Who came from living worlds, though in that
    house
There was a pensive figure in one seat,
Which the pale mother, with her tear-stained
    eyes,
Looked on and drooped her head ; the father,
    too.

When he stepped forth upon his homeward path
('T was a short saunter to the village church)
A change was in the sky ; a wild wind blew ;
The frost was tired of silence, and now played
A merry battle-march with the light snow
That whirled across the road in dizzy sport.
From the low hills that hem the meadows in
The Sexton heard the music of the pines—
A sudden gush of sounds, as when a flock
Of startled birds are beating through the air
And tossing off the snow from their quick wings.
Then came a heavier blast than all before,
And beat upon the cheerful Sexton's front.

THE CONCORD SEXTON'S STORY

He ploughed along the way—nor fence nor shrub,
And a dark curtain in the air; the stars
Were flickering, as the distant light-boat moored
Shifts to the pilot's eye, each breaking wave.

His eye, not eager, sought the willow arch,—
"A little onward to the bridge," he thought,—
And turning beat his stout arms on his breast,
Then turned and faced the wintry surge again.
One step—and then his foot sank through; the
    edge
It was of the deep Brook that wandered down
The dreary meadows, sinuous in its course.
The Sexton's feet slipped o'er the glassy plate;
He was across—across the meadow Brook.
He sank upon the snow and breathed a prayer.

And one dark. warning figure, wintry Death,
Stood on the bank and said with gentle voice:
"Yes, now across the Brook thy feet have come—
The deep black Brook; 't was never known to
    freeze,
Yet has upborne thee on its icy scale,
Where but a feather's weight had turned the
    beam:
Yet by no chance—since this a lesson is
To teach thee, if the burial and the tomb
Consign to rest the palsied shapes of Life,

How grand that hour must be when the bright
    soul,
Led by my hand, draws near to the deep stream
Across whose icy flow no mortal walks—
In whose still, unvexed depths the hosts of men,
Each other following, sink without return."

There stood a laborer's cottage not far off,
Where the day's toil was over, and they sat,
The family, about the crackling fire
In merry mood, and heard the spinning wheels
Hum like a swarm of bees in Summer-time,
For all the wind's loud bluster and the cold
That like a cunning thief crept round the hut.
They sudden hear a lamentable sound—
A voice in wild despair imploring aid.
The voice comes from the meadow; then his dog
The laborer calls, and, muffling in his frock,
He finds the Sexton by the Brook sunk down,
And stiffening like the cold and icy night.

Next day they traced the hardy Sexton's steps,
And found that but one narrow arch across
The meadow Brook the spanning ice had thrown,
As if, in sport, to try its secret powers;
And there the Sexton crossed—that little arch
Left him alive to guide the funeral train

That from that friendly house came forth in woe.
It taught this lesson—that in common hours
There hides deep meaning and a sudden fear;
Nor need we track the deserts of the Pole
To meet the sight of Death and Life's dark night.

THE MOUNTAINS

TOYS for the angry lightning in its play—
    Summits and peaks and crests untrod and
      steep!
Ye precipices where the eyes delay,
    Sheer gulfs that madly plunge to valleys deep,
Overhung valleys, curtained by dark forms,
Ye! nourished by the energetic storms—
    I seek you, lost in spellbound, shuddering sleep!

Within your rifts hang gem-like, crystal stars;
    Eyeless by day, they glitter through the nights;
Full-zoned Venus and red-visaged Mars,
    And that serenest Jupiter's grand lights,
Peer o'er your terrible eminences near,
But throned too high to stoop with mortal fear—
    Dreading you not, ye ocean-stemming heights!

Your awful forms pale wandering mists surround;
    Dim clouds enfold you in funereal haze;
In the white-frosted winters ye abound,
    And your vast fissures with the frost-work glaze,
Slippery and careless of ascending feet,
Holding out violent death; not thus may meet
    The Olympians, mortals with unshrinking gaze.

THE MOUNTAINS

The fierce Bald Eagle builds amid your caves,
 Shrieks fearless in your lonely places, where
Only his brothers of the wind make waves,
 Sweeping with lazy pinions the swift air;
Far, far below, the stealthy wolf retreats,
The fox his various victims crafty greets;
 Breeze-knighted birds alone make you their lair.

Sometimes in the green valley peasants stand,
 Shading their glance at midday as they pass,
And wonder at such beacons in the land—
 Bending again their eyes upon the grass.
Ye heaven-high mountains! deign to stand alone.
Only the airy amphitheatre own—
 Only the shapely clouds, the snows' drear mass!

What are ye, grand, unuttered words of Power?
 Why stand you thus, balancing only earth?
Shall not an echo wake, an untold hour
 Stir in your cavernous breasts a giant birth?
Shall ye not answer to the roar of seas,
Send back your greetings to the running breeze?
 Mountains, I hear you in your mighty mirth!

HYMN OF THE EARTH

MY highway is unfeatured Air,
　My consorts are the sleepless Stars,
And men my giant arms upbear,
　My arms unstained and free from scars.
I rest forever on my way,
　Rolling around the happy Sun;
My children love the sunny day,
　But noon and night to me are one.

My heart has pulses like their own;
　I am their Mother, and my veins,
Though built of the enduring stone,
Thrill, as do theirs, with godlike pains.
The Forests and the Mountains high,
　The foaming Ocean, and the Springs,
The Plains—O pleasant Company!
　My voice through all your anthem rings.

Ye are so cheerful in your minds,
　Content to smile, content to share—
My being in your chorus finds
　The echo of the spheral air.
No leaf may fall, no pebble roll,
　No drop of water lose the road;
The issues of the general Soul
　Are mirrored in its round abode.

TO THE POETS

THEY who sing the deeds of men
  From the earth upraise their fame—
Monuments in marble pen,
  Keeping ever sweet their name;
    Tell me, Poets, do I hear
    What you sing, with pious ear?

They who sing the maiden's kiss
  And the silver sage's thought,
Loveliness of inward bliss
  Or a graver learning taught,
    Tell me, are your skies and streams
    Real, or the shape of dreams?

Many rainy days must go,
  Many clouds the sun obscure;
But your verses clearer show,
  And your lovely thoughts more pure;
    Mortals are we, but you are
    Burning keenly like a star.

THE WOODMAN

This poem is made up from three long ones, written at his Ponkatasset
cottage, but recalling the poet's own experience as a woodman, while he
lived in the village and spent days chopping in Britton's woods, toward
Lincoln.

DEEP in the forest stands he there;
   His gleaming axe cuts crashing through
(While Winter whistles in the air)
   The oak's tough trunk and flexile bough.

Above the wood the ravens call;
   Their dusky murmurs fill the space.
Small snowbirds toss above the wall,
   And flickering shadows span the place.

Naught but the drifting cloud o'erhead,
   Naught but the stately pines off there;
A glaze o'er all the picture 's spread—
   A medium that far suns prepare.

In distant groves the foxhound bays,
   Where faintly strokes of axes beat;
The thin snow drives across the ways,
   Untrampled by the Woodman's feet.

THE WOODMAN

Within each tree the circles are
  That years have drawn with patient art;
Against its life he maketh war
  And stills the beating of its heart.

The rough pitch-pine, with scaly stem,
  Crashes with thunder to the ground;
Its rich red mail is naught to him —
  Within the pile its worth is found

The tough white oak commands his eye,
  Which sees it in the sawmill's power;
Its leaves, fern-colored, rustling fly —
  Its winding limbs have had their hour.

He must beware the dulling stone
  Where drifts the snow, nor swerve his hand;
A hair shall make his axe atone
  For his mad carnage in the land.

When handsome noon divides the day,
  Behind the pile he sits content;
He needs no fire: the sun's kind ray
  Tempers the stinging element.

He opes the pail stored with corn-bread,
  And frosty cake of homely art,
And apples that last Autumn shed,
  With russet leaves, from his good heart.

Fearless the snow-white bunting came
  To peck the crumbs that near him fell;
No need to give that bird a name,
  He knew its pouting breast so well.

His brother woodmen tramp the road
  Silent and staring, striding by;
For onward is their near abode,
  Where, with the noon, they hungry hie.

When half the afternoon is o'er
  He builds his cord; a sharpened stake
At each end driven through his floor
  Secures the structures he must make.

Upon that floor a leafy bed
  Conceals where grass or green moss grows;
The rugged trees their branches spread,
  And lattice-in his sky that glows.

As with a flood of amber light
  Day's candle sinks below the west;
The woods around him smile "Good night";
  'T is time for home—'t is time for rest.

He leaves the wood when twilight burns
  Dim on his solitary way;
Then into farmers' lanes he turns,
  Or on the highroad whistles gay,

THE WOODMAN

Where broad-shod sleds have creased the snow
  And robbed the Winter of its tint;
There rise the gray barns, and the low
  Rain-painted house begins to glint.

He drops his axe, the kitchen seeks,
  Where from his hearth steams forth the tea;
And pinches his fat baby's cheeks,
  And tells his wife of you and me.

His wife has talked with neighbor Sue,
  And little Patty's cold is worse;
The pump is frozen;—thus what 's new
  And what is old they each rehearse.

The bold North Wind his cannon fires,
  Sweeping the pines; the smoke flies fast;
They shake,—the pointed, twinkling spires,—
  While o'er the field ploughs the cold blast.

THE POET

EVEN in the winter's depth the Pine-tree stands
  With a perpetual summer in its leaves;
So stands the Poet, with his open hands—
  Nor care nor sorrow him of life bereaves.

Though others pine for piles of glittering gold,
  A cloudless sunset furnishes him enough;
His garments never can grow thin or old;
  His way is always smooth, though seeming rough.

For though his sorrows fall like icy rain,
  Straightway the clouds do open where he goes,
And e'en his tears become a precious gain—
  'T is thus the hearts of mortals that he knows.

The figures of his landscape may appear
  Sordid or poor; their colors he can paint;
And, listening to the hooting, he can hear
  Such harmonies as never sung the Saint.

'T is in his heart where dwells his pure desire,
  Let other outward lot be dark or fair;
In coldest weather there is inward fire—
  In fogs he breathes a clear, celestial air.

92

THE POET

Some shady wood in summer is his room;
　Behind a rock in winter he can sit;
The wind shall sweep his chamber, and his loom —
　The birds and insects weave content at it.

Above his head the broad sky's beauties are;
　Beneath, the ancient carpet of the earth:
A glance at that unveileth every star;
　The other, joyfully it feels his birth.

So sacred is his calling that no thing
　Of disrepute can follow in his path;
His destiny 's too high for sorrowing;
　The mildness of his lot is kept from wrath.

So let him stand, resigned to his estate;
　Kings cannot compass it, nor nobles have:
They are the children of some handsome fate,
　He of himself is beautiful and brave.

REPENTANCE

A CLOUD upon the day is lying,
　　A cloud of care, a cloud of sorrow,
That will not speed away for sighing,
　　That will not lift upon the morrow;
And yet it is not gloom I carry
　　To shade a world else framed in lightness;
It is not Sorrow that doth tarry
　　To veil the joyous sky of brightness.

Then tell me what it is, thou Nature,
　　That of all earth art queen supremest!
Give to my grief distinctest feature,
　　Thou who art ever to me nearest!
Because my lot has no distinction,
　　And unregarded I am standing,
A pilgrim wan, without dominion,
　　A shipwrecked mariner just landing.

Resolve for me, ye prudent sages,
　　Why I am tasked without a reason;
Or penetrate the lapse of ages,
　　And show where is my summer season.

94

REPENTANCE

For let the sky be blue above me,
  Or softest breezes lift the forest,
I still, uncertain, wander to thee—
  Thou who the lot of man deplorest.

I will not strive for Fortune's gilding,
  But still the disappointment follow;
Seek steadily the pasture's wilding,
  Nor grasp a satisfaction hollow.

THE LONELY ROAD

This is the "old Carlisle Road," leading through the Estabrook country," celebrated by Thoreau, and where his Canada lynx was killed. When Channing lived at Hillside, as he called his Ponkatasset house, to this wild region was an easy stroll across pastures and a brook. This particular stroll was taken in the winter of 1845-46, in company with William Tappan, husband of his early friend Caroline Sturgis.

NO track had worn the lone, deserted road,
  Save where the fox had leaped from wall to
    wall;
There were the swelling, glittering piles of snow,
Up even with the walls; and, save the crow
Who lately had been pecking barberries,
No other sign of life beyond ourselves.
We strayed along; beneath our feet the lane
Creaked at each pace, and soon we stood content
Where the old cellar of a house had been,
Out of which now a fruit-tree wags its top.

Some scraggy orchards hem the landscape round—
A forest of sad apple-trees unpruned,
And then a newer orchard—pet of him
Who in his dotage kept this lonely place.
In this wild scene, this shut-in orchard dell,
Men like ourselves once dwelt by roaring fires—
Loved this still spot, nor had a further wish.

THE LONELY ROAD

A little wall, half falling, bounds a square
Where choicer fruit-trees showed the garden's
    pride,
Now crimsoned by the sumach, whose red cones
Displace the colors of the cultured growth.

I know not how it is that in these scenes
There is a desolation so complete;
It tarries with me after I have passed,
And the dense growth of woodland, or a sight
Of distant cottages, or landscapes wide,
Cannot obscure the dreary, cheerless thought.
I people the void scene with Fancy's eye;
Her children do not live too long for me;
They vibrate in the house whose walls I rear,
(The mansion as themselves), the fugitives
Of my intent, in this soft winter day.

Nor will I scatter these faint images,
Idle as shadows that the tall reeds cast
Over the silent ice, beneath the moon;
For in these lonely haunts where Fancy dwells,
And, evermore creating, weaves a veil
In which all this that we call life abides,
There must be deep retirement from the day;
And in these shadowy vistas we shall meet
Sometime the very phantom of ourselves.

A long farewell, thou dim and silent spot !
Where serious Winter sleeps, or the soft hour
Of some half-dreamy Autumn afternoon ;
And may no idle feet tread thy domain,
But only men to contemplation vowed—
Still, as ourselves, creators of the Past.

THE BARREN MOORS

This tract also is a part of the Estabrook region, and even nearer
to Hillside than the road just pictured.

ON your bare rocks, O barren Moors!
  On your bare rocks I love to lie;
They stand like crags upon the shores,
  Or clouds upon a placid sky.
Across these spaces desolate
  The fox pursues his lonely way;
These solitudes can fairly sate
  The passage of my loneliest day.

Like desert islands far at sea,
  Where not a ship can ever land,
These dim uncertainties to me
  For something veritable stand:
A serious place, distinct from all
  Which busy life delights to feel;
I stand in this deserted hall,
  And here the wounds of Time conceal.

No friend's cold eye, or sad delay,
  Shall vex me now, where not a sound
Falls on the ear, and every day
  Is soft as silence most profound.

No more upon these distant wolds
The agitating world can come;
A single pensive thought upholds
The arches of this dreamy home.

Within the sky above, one thought
Replies to you, O barren Moors!
Between I stand—a creature taught
To stand between two silent floors.

FIELD-BIRDS' NESTS

BEYOND the speeding brook I went,
    Beyond the fields my course I bent,
Where on the height an oak-grove stands,
And hemlocks thick, like iron bands.
Then by the marsh and by the Pond,
Though I had wandered o't beyond,
Never before saw I those eight,
Yes, eight birds' nests, now desolate.

Each nest was filled with snow and leaves—
Such nest as some small songster weaves;
Yet pleasant was their strange array,
Those little homes of yesterday;
So frail their building that the wind
To airy journeys had consigned,
Had not each architect displayed
The quiet cunning of his trade.

On some small twig each house was laid,
That every breath from heaven swayed;
The nests swing easy as the bush—
In vain the wind on these may push:

CARL A. RUDISILL LIBRARY
LENOIR RHYNE COLLEGE

A twig 's the rock on which they stand
As firm as acres of deep land—
With grass and sticks together piled,
Secure as stately palace tiled.

Another summer comes the bird,
And sweetly swelling song is heard;
She hops into her little home—
Her mate as merrily doth come.

Ye men who pass a wretched life,
Consumed with care, consumed with strife,
Whose gloom grows deeper day by day,
The audience at a tiresome play!
Who build the stately palaces
Where only endless gilding is,
Who riot in perpetual show,
In dress and wine and costly woe!

Who haunt the stony city's street,
Surrounded by a thousand feet,
With weary wrinkles in your brows
And faltering penance in your vows:
Think of the little field-bird's nest!
Can you not purchase such a rest!
A twig, some straws, a dreamy moor—
The same some summers going o'er.

THE ARCHED STREAM

IT went within my inmost heart
    That overhanging arch to see!
The liquid stream became a part
    Of my internal harmony.
So gladly rushed the full stream through,
    Pleased with the measure of its flow,
So burst its gladness on the view,
    It made a song of mirth below.

Yet gray were those o'erarching stones,
    And sere and dry the fringing grass;
And mournful the remembered tones
    That out of Autumn's bosom pass;
And o'er the bridge the heavy road,
    Where creaks the wain with burdened cheer;
But gayly, from this low abode,
    Leaped out the merry brook so clear.

Then Nature said : "My child, to thee
    From this gray arch shall Beauty flow;
Thou art a pleasing thing to me,
    And freely in my meadows go!
Thy verse shall gush as freely on;
    Some Poet yet may sit thereby
And cheer himself within the sun
    My life has kindled in thine eye."

POEMS OF THE HEART

I. ODE TO EMERSON

IF we should rake the bottom of the sea
  For its best treasures,
  And heap our measures,—
If we should ride upon the winds, and be
  Partakers of their flight
  By day and through the night,—
Intent upon this business, to find gold,
Yet were thy story perfectly untold.

Such waves of wealth are rolled up in thy soul,—
  Such swelling argosies
  Laden with Time's supplies,—
Such pure, delicious wine shines in the bowl,
  We could drink evermore
  Upon the glittering shore;
Drink of the pearl-dissolvèd, brilliant cup—
Be madly drunk and drown our thirsting up!

This vessel, richly chased about the brim
  With golden emblems, is
  The utmost art of bliss;
With figures of the azure Gods, who swim
  In the enchanted Sea
  Contrived for Deity,

104

Floating in rounded shells of purple hue;
The sculptor died in carving this so true.

Some dry, uprooted saplings we have seen
　　　Pretend to even
　　　Thy grove of Heaven—
A sacred forest, where the foliage green
　　　Breathes music of mild lutes,
　　　Or silver-coated flutes,
On the concealing winds—that can convey
Never their tone to the rude ear of Day.

Some weary-footed mortals we have found
　　　Adventuring after thee:
　　　They, rooted, as a tree
Pursues the swift breeze o'er a rocky ground—
　　　Thy grand, imperial flight
　　　Swept thee as far from sight
As sweeps the movement of a southern blast
Across the heated Gulf, and bends the mast.

The circles of thy thought shine vast as stars;
　　　No glass shall round them,
　　　No plummet sound them;
They hem the observer like bright, steel-wrought
　　　bars;
　　　Yet limpid as the sun,
　　　Or as bright waters run

From coldest fountain of the Alpine springs,
Or diamonds richly set in royal rings.

The piercing of thy soul scorches our thought,
    As great fires burning,
    Or sunlight turning
Into a focus: in thy meshes caught,
    Our palpitating minds
    Show stupid, as coarse hinds';
So strong and composite through all thy powers
The Intellect divine serenely towers.

This heavy castle's gates no man can ope,
    Unless the Lord doth will
    To prove his skill,
And read the fates hid in his horoscope;
    No man may enter there
    But first shall kneel in prayer
And orisons to superior Gods shall say—
Powers of old time, unveiled in this our day.

The smart and pathos of our suffering race
    Bears thee no harm;
    Thy muscular arm
The daily ills of living doth efface;
    The sources of that spring
    From whence thy instincts wing
Are sounded not by lines of sordid Day;
Enclosed with inlaid wall 's thy virtue's way.

POEMS OF THE HEART

In city's street how often shall we hear,
    "It is a period
    Deprived of every God—
A time of indecision, and Doom 's near."
    While foolish altercation
    Threatens to break our nation;
All men turned talkers, and much good forgot—
With scores of curious troubles we know not.

We never heard thee babble in this wise,
    Thou age-creator,
    And clear debater
Of that which this good Present underlies;
    Thy course is better kept
    Than where the dreamers slept—
Thy sure meridian 's taken by the sun;
Thy compass points as true as waters run.

In vain for us to say what thou hast been
    To our occasion—
    This flickering nation,
This stock of people from an English kin;
    And he who led the van,—
    The frozen Puritan,—
We thank thee for thy patience with his faith,
That chill, delusive poison, mixed for death.

Within thy book the world is plainly set
    Before our vision;
    Thou keen Physician!
We find there wisely writ what we have met
    Along our dusty path,
    Or o'er the aftermath,
Where natures once world-daring held the scythe,
Nor paid to superstition a mean tithe.

We need not search for men in Sidney's times,
    Nor Raleigh's fashion
    And Herbert's passion;
For us these are but dry, preservèd limes.
    There is ripe fruit to-day
    Hangs yellow in display
Upon the waving guerdon of the bough:
The graceful Gentleman lives for us now.

Neither must thou turn back to Angelo,
    Who Rome commanded,
    And, single-handed,
Was Architect, Poet, and bold Sculptor too;
    Behold a better thing,
    When the pure mind can sing,
When true Philosophy is linked with verse,
And moral laws in rhyme themselves rehearse!

POEMS OF THE HEART

Great Persons are the epochs of the race;
    Then royal Nature
    Takes form and feature,
And careless handles the surrounding space;
    An Age is vain and thin,
    A pageant of gay sin,
Without heroic response from the soul
Through which the tides diviner amply roll.

The pins of Custom have not pierced through thee;
    A perfect charmer
    'S thy shining armor;
Even the hornets of Divinity
    Allow thee a brief space;
    And thy thought hath a place
Along the Scholar's well-selected shelves,
Where the gray Sage of various wisdom delves.

So moderate in thy lessons, and so wise,
    To foes so courteous,
    To friends so duteous,
And hospitable in the neighbors' eyes—
    Thy thoughts have fed the lamp
    In Learning's polished camp;
And who suspects thee of this well-earned fame?
Or meditates on thy renownèd name?[1]

[1] Written in 1846 or earlier, this question could be asked,
but now is superfluous.

When thou dost pass below thy forest shade,
 The branches drooping
 Enfold thee, stooping
Above thy figure, and form thus a glade;
 The flowers admire thee pass;
 In much content the grass
Awaits the pressure of thy firm-set feet;
The bird for thee sends out his greeting sweet.

Upon the River thou dost float at peace,
 Or on the Ocean
 Feelest its motion;
Of every natural form thou hast the lease—
 Because thy way lies there
 Where it is good or fair:
Thou hast perception, learning, and much art,
Propped by the columns of a stately heart.

From deepest mysteries thy goblet fills;
 The wines do murmur
 That Nature warmed her,
When she, from must, was pressing out the hills,
 And plains that near us lie,
 The foldings of the sky—
Whate'er within the horizon's range there is,
From Hades' caldron to the blue God's bliss.

110

We may no more—so we might sing fore'er,
    Thy thought recalling;
    Thus waters falling
Over great cataracts from their lakes do bear
    A power that is divine,
    And bends their stately line.
All but thy Beauty these cold verses have—
All but thy Music, organ-mellowed nave!

II. HAWTHORNE IN THE OLD MANSE

THERE in the old gray house, whose end we see
Half peeping through the golden willow's veil,
Whose graceful twigs make foliage through the
    year,
My Hawthorne dwelt—a scholar of rare worth.
New England's Chaucer, Hawthorne fitly lives,
The gentlest man that kindly Nature drew.

His tall, compacted figure, ably strung
To urge the Indian chase or guide the way—
Softly reclining 'neath the aged elm,
Like some still rock looked out upon the scene,
As much a part of Nature as itself.

The passing Fisher saw this idle man
Thus lying solitary 'neath the elm;
And as he plied with lusty arm his oar,
Shooting upon the tranquil glass below
The old Red Bridge,—and farther on the stream
To those still coves where the great prizes swim,—
Asked of himself this question—why that man
Thus idly on the bank o'erlooked the stream?
Then by the devious light, at twilight's close,
He read the *Twice-told Tales*—nor dreamt the
    mind
Thus idly musing by the river's side
Had gathered and stored up from Nature's fields
This golden grain.
             From out the sunny brake,
Or where the Great Fields glimmer in the sun,
Such mystic influence came to Hawthorne's soul,
That from the air and from the liquid day
He drank the subtle image of deep life.
And when the grand and cumbrous winter rose,
Sealing the face of Nature as with stone,
He sat within the Manse, and filled the place
With all the wealth of summer, like a sun.
Still were these plains more sacred in my eyes
That furnished treasure for his kingly purse.

POEMS OF THE HEART

III. COUNT JULIAN
Another Sketch of Hawthorne

As in some stately grove of singing pines
One tree, more marked than all, decisive rears
Its grand, aspiring figure to the sky,
Remote from those beneath, and o'er whose top
The first faint light of dawn familiar plays,
So in Count Julian's face there was the soul
Of something deeper than the general heart—
Some memory more near to other worlds,
Time's recollection, and the storied Past.

His pure, slight form had a true Grecian charm,
Soft as the willow o'er the river swaying,
Yet sinewy, and capable of action—
Such grace as in Apollo's figure lay
When he was moving the still world with light.
About his forehead clustered rich black curls,
Medusa-like ; they charmed the student's eye.
Those soft, still hazel orbs Count Julian had
Looked dream-like forth on the familiar day-
Yet eloquent, and full of luminous force
Sweetly humane,—that had no harshness known,—
Unbroken eyes, where love forever dwelt.

This art of Nature which surrounded him,
This made Count Julian what he was to me-

Which neither time nor place nor poet's pen
Nor sculptor's chisel e'er can mould again.

IV. ALCOTT

LIGHT from a better land!
Fire from a burning brand!
Though in this cold, sepulchral clime,
Chained to an unambitious time,
    Thou slowly moulderest;
Yet cheer that great and lowly heart,
Prophetic eye and sovereign part!
And be thy fortune greatly blest,
And by some greater gods confest,
    With a sublimer rest!

Strike on, nor still thy golden lyre,
That sparkles with Olympian fire!
And be thy word the soul's desire
    Of this unthinking land!
Nor shall thy voyage of glory fail;
Its sea thou sweepest—set thy sail!
Though fiercely rave the heaviest gale,
    It shall not swerve thy hand.

Born for a fate whose secret none
Hath looked upon beneath Earth's sun—
Child of the High, the Only One!
    Thy glories sleep secure!

114

On Heaven's coast thy mounting wave
Shall dash beyond the unknown grave,
And cast its spray to warn and save
Some other barks that moor.

V. THOREAU (AT WALDEN)

It is not far beyond the village church
(After we pass the wood that skirts the road),
A Lake, the blue-eyed Walden, that doth smile
Most tenderly upon its neighbor pines;
And they, as if to recompense this love,
In double beauty spread their branches forth.
This Lake hath tranquil loveliness and breadth,
And of late years hatn added to its charms;
For One, attracted to its pleasant edge,
Has built him there a little Hermitage,
Where with much piety he passes life.

But more than either Lake or forest's depths
This man has in himself: a tranquil man,
With sunny sides, where well the fruit is ripe—
Good front and resolute bearing to his life,
And some serener virtues, which control
This rich exterior prudence; virtues high,
That in the principles of things are set,
Great by their nature, and consigned to him,
Who like a faithful merchant does account
To God for what he spends, and in what way.

Thrice happy art thou, Walden: in thyself
(Such purity is in thy limpid springs);
In those green shores which do reflect in thee;
And in this man who dwells upon thine edge—
A holy man within a Hermitage.
May all good showers fall gently into thee!
May thy surrounding forest long be spared!
And may this Dweller on thy tranquil shores
There lead a life of deep tranquillity!
Pure as thy waters, handsome as thy shores,
And with those virtues that are like the stars.

VI. ELIZABETH HOAR

BELIEVE that I, a humble worshipper,
 Who in soiled weeds along this pathway 's
  going,
To one of nobler kind may minister,
 His lowly hope in these faint words bestowing:
O Lady, that my words for thee were more!
But I have not the right to richer store.

Thou art of finer mould—thy griefs are proof;
 Only those nearest to the sun do burn,
While we sit merry underneath the roof,
 And vainly to those larger empires turn;
Had I been heir of brightness, as art thou,
Then might a sorrow seal my rounded brow.

POEMS OF THE HEART

VII. TO THOSE ADDRESSED

O BAND of Friends! ye breathe within this
    space,
And the rough finish of a humble man
By your kind touches rises into Art.
I cannot lose a line ye bend to trace;
Your figures bear into the azure deeps
A little frail contentment of my own;
And in your eyes I read how sunshine lends
A golden color to the dusty weed,
That droops its tints where the soiled Pilgrims
    tread.

VIII. THE ESTRANGED FRIEND

THE day has passed—I never may return;
    Twelve circling years have run since first I
    came
    And kindled the pure truth of Friendship's
    flame;
Alone remain these ashes in the urn.
Vainly for light the taper may I turn;
    Thy hand is closed, as for these years the same,
    And of the substance naught is but the name—
No more a hope, no more a ray to burn.

But once more, in the pauses of thy joy,
  Remember him who sought thee in his youth,
And with the old reliance of the boy
  Asked for thy treasures in the guise of Truth.
The air is thick with sighs,—the shaded sun
Creeps from the hillside, and the day is done.

IX. UNFAITHFUL FRIENDSHIP

The sonnet just given was written, says the manuscript. "in the road
between L. and S.," which I take to be Lenox and Stockbridge. The
year must have been 1845 or 1846. This less poetic expostulation may
explain the causes of the separation, which was only on the poet's side,
I fancy, knowing both.

You recollect our younger years, my Friend,
And rambles in the country; life could lend
No choicer volumes for the Student's eye.
You must remember that it was not I
Who brought conclusion to these rambling
    moods—
Our joint connection with the streams and woods:
'T was ever thou—thou who art steeped in
    thought,
Subtle and dexterous, wise—but good for naught.
I mean no harm; thou art not good for me—
Thou reasonest, demandest; I ask *thee*.

Thou didst not know that Friendship is a kiss—
Not thought, philosophy,—some Sage's bliss,—

118

But a strange fire that falleth from above;
The gods have named this star-shower Human Love.
No—thou wert blinded; thou saidst, "Friend,
    forbear!
Do not come nigh—my heart thou canst not share."
(My heart, alas! I gave that all away.)
I do not love thee near me; bide thy day!
Fashion I seek, and whirling gayety,
Not thou, sad Poet! what art thou to me?
More—I have married an angelic wife,
Who wreathes with roses my enchanted life;
Thou art superfluous—come not thou too near!
Let us be distant friends, and no more dear.

"What were thy eager fancies, running o'er
Half of the world? I anchor near the shore:
Thy silly jests for idlers' ears are fit,
And only silence complements thy wit.
I love thee at arm's-length; my quarantine
Declares pacific measures, and divine.
I would it were not so—poor, helpless thing,
That like a blue jay can but shriek or sing
Those lamentable ditties that refuse
To call themselves productions of the Muse!
Nay! walk not with me in the curling wood!
I stride abroad in quest of solitude.
I love my friends far off; when they come near,
Too warm! too warm the crowded atmosphere."

119

X. TO ROSALIE

This name in the first manuscript is "Rosaline." Channing calls this "a purely imaginary portraiture," but this may be doubted.

GIRL so beautiful,
   So sweet! I dare not love;
Girl so dutiful
   That my heart did move
   With pure delight
And tranquil worship at thy sight!

I might love when passion dances
   In a dark, entrancing eye,
Answering to my fond glances—
   Answering I know not why:
   But that modest, simple child,
   Figure holy, aspect mild,
   With no thought of me or mine,
   The angelic Rosaline!
   As the beauty flowed o'er me,
   Noble Maiden! born with thee,
   Only could I wonder long—
   For thee frame this feeble song.

Then I knelt before her beauty,
   And I woke from idle longing;
Made it my peculiar duty
   With this child, to Love belonging,

Her to lead in wood and dell,
Where the streams conceal their spell
 In the sleeping solitudes,
  Where an ancient silence nods
 In the old, complacent woods,
  Haunt of unpretending Gods:
And where'er the secret bird
With such melody is heard,
 As a dewy rose-leaf falling,
Loosely in the summer wind,
 Or the twilight fancies calling
Far the buried sun behind,
When on high a vesper bell,
 Softly tolling day's declining,
In the mountains sounding well,
 Answers to a heart repining;
Or a sigh of the wind-harp's tongue
On a silken zephyr sung.

Be the season cool or warm,
May it soothe her with its charm!
In gay blossoms Spring enfold her,
'Mid rich flowers may Summer hold her!
With ripe fruit brown Autumn bless her,
With brave cheer white Winter dress her!
 And more, may I
 Resist the force of ever tie,

121

And on this spotless errand bent,
With a duty abstinent,
  Vow to her the steadfast heart,
Silent tongue, and sleepless thought,
  Vow to her the spoils of Art,
And the gold the mind has brought
From her rivers in the Reason,
To regild the faded season—
Vow them all!
And her my mistress call,
Whom to love were hopeless folly—
Maiden mild, and pure and holy,
Whom to love was not for me,
But to worship sacredly.

XI. TO EDWARD EMERSON (THREE YEARS OLD)

(1847)

A LITTLE Boy,
To be his parents' joy;
A tender three-year-old,
Shut in a shapely fold,
Whose trustful eye
Draws a great circle of new sky!

  That eye is blue
As loved Italia's heaven,
  Or the mid-ocean's hue,
Or Mediterranean even;

Or the bright petal of a star-shaped flower,
Autumnal Aster's or fringed Gentian's dower,
Or the just gods' cerulean hall.
How shone this eye on us at all?
How is it here,
Smiling blue above the bier
Of the dead Autumn flower,
In my November hour!

Child of the good Divinity!
Thou child of One
Who smiles on me like a most friendly sun!
How gaze our wondering eyes at thee,
Thou whom the God has anchored
In a bare plain, from the clear sea
Of his creative pleasure!
Moored thee, to measure
The fathoms of the sense
In this hard present tense!
Child of the azure sky,
Who hast outdone it in thine eye,
That trellised window in unfathomed blue!
Child of the Mid-world sweet and true,
Child of the combing, crystal spheres
Throned above this salt pool of tears!
Child of Immortality,
Why hast thou come to cheat the Destiny!

By the sweet mouth, half parted in a smile,
That dimpled never in some Indian isle,
 By upright figure and fat cheek,
 And by thy creamy voice so meek,
 By all thou art,—
 By the pat beating of thy crisscross
  heart,—
How couldst thou light ont his plain, homespun
  shore ɪ
And, not upon thy own aërial riding,
Fall down to Earth, where turbid sadly pour
The old, perpetual rivers of backsliding.

  Since thou art here, and fast
  On our autumnal ball—
Renounce, if possible, the mighty air-spanned
  Hall !
 Its chalice of imperial nectar,
  Vases of transparent porphyry,
 Amethystine rings of splendor,
  Bright footstools of chalcedony—
  The alabaster bed,
Where in the plume of seraph sunk thy
  head,
To the full-sounding organ of the Sphere,
By the smooth, hyaline finger of thy peer
  So amorously played !
Stay with us, if thou art not too much afraid !

POEMS OF THE HEART

Lap thyself here in beds of roses,
  Bathe thee in Spring's cosmetic time,
Waken old Autumn where his head reposes,
  Or kiss the cheek of Summer in her prime!
Turn the dark Winter night to day.
      Stay with us,
      Play with us;
   Go not, go not away!

    Here are prickly chestnuts
      That tinkle as they fall,
    And oily meat of walnuts,
      And cones of the pitch-pine tall;
    By terraces with alders sown
      Along the fleet brook's grassy side,
    Thou mayst sail thy skiff alone,
      Where the amber waters glide;
      Fix a blue jay's scream
        For the whistle of thy car!
      Costliest music for thy **dream**
        Be tap of the hard-billed woodpecker!
Ambrosia 's in the tip of the Columbine,
And in the red fox-grape 's a tartish wine.

    Be those blue eyes
      Our only atmosphere!
    For in them lies
What is than Earth, than distant Heaven, more
      dear.

XII. A PRAYER

To Thy continual Presence, in me wrought,
    Vainly might I, a fallen creature, say
Through Thee, Thou essence of Creation's thought,
    That I partake the blessedness of Day ;
That on my verse might fall Thy healing dew !
And all its faults obscure, its charms renew.

I praise Thee—not because Thou needest
    praise
(What were my thanks ?   Thou needest not my
    lays)—
Yet will I praise Thee—for Thou art the fire
That sparkles on the strings of my dark lyre.

Sole Majesty ! around us softly flowing,
Unseen, yet in the common sunset glowing !
Fate of the Universe ! the Tide of things !
Sacred alike to all beneath Thy wings.

If Passion's trance lay on my writing clear,
Then should I see Thee, evident and near ;
Passion—that breath of Instinct, and the key
Of Thy dominions, untold Mystery !

POEMS OF THE HEART

XIII. TO MY COMPANIONS

YE heavy-hearted Mariners
  Who sail this shore—
Ye patient! ye who labor
  Sitting at the sweeping oar,
And see afar the flashing sea-gulls play
On the free waters, and the glad, bright Day
    Twine with his hand the spray—
  From out your dreariness,
  From your heart-weariness,
  I speak; for I am yours,
  On these gray shores.

In vain—I know not, Mariners,
  What cliffs these are
That high uplift their smooth, dark fronts
  And sadly round us bar;
I do imagine that the free clouds play
Above those eminent heights; that somewhere
    Day
    Rides his triumphant way
  Over our stern oblivion;
  And hath his pure dominion.
  But see no path thereout
  To free from doubt.

POEMS OF MATURITY
AND AGE

THE POET'S DEJECTION

THERE are no tears to shed; the heart is dry,
  And the thin leaves of hope fall from the
      bough,
Rustling and sere—all winter in the tree.
Some smarting pain, some swiftly shooting ill,
Needless alarm or interrupted fear,
Chances and changes, and the soul's despair,
All we can suffer—all that we deplore
Were happier far than these unmoving hours,
When I sit silent on the sandy shore,
Silent, uncomforted, hapless, and lone.
Why are ye bright, why are ye sunny, days,
With the blue sky that arches over all,
And the sweet wind that with a breath of love
Touches the golden hilltops till they smile?
  I murmur from my soul its cherished thoughts,
All I have known or suffered; and I ask
The friends I love to come and sit with me,
And call to memory for their cheerful smiles.
They cannot answer me; no visions rise;
And in such ebbing hours life passes as
A faint and burdened man, whose aching feet
Support him tottering o'er the sandy wastes
In the unlidded blaze of Afric's eye.

Oh, little feel the gay, remorseless crowd,
Intent on pleasures, of the poet's care;
The path he treads must be by them untrod;
His destiny a veil, his heart—unsealed;
While all around him swims dancing in joy,
And smiling faces and soft azure skies,
Tantalus-like that he shall never touch,
Look in across the dead sea of his life,
Like goblin masks, fleshless and cold and pale.

Would that the heart might break, the mind
    decease,
Or ever these dark hours that do not move,
Sullen and stagnant as the marshy pool
Whose side the rank sedge crowds, while the green
    ooze
Spreads o'er the shallows its soft, slimy veil!
Will the prevented waters ne'er o'erflow,
Burst down their muddy dams, and, leaping clear,
Dance through the valleys like a song of joy?
Is there imprisoned winter through my heart,
Frozen to its centre like an icy shroud?
Am I embraced in stone or filled with dust?
Tell me, kind destinies, who rule our days!
In vain; ye ne'er reveal it. There 's no soul
Within us that applauds these sullen hours.

THE POET'S DEJECTION

Yet let me suffer with a patient thought;
'T is but another turning of the tide
That from the far-off ocean of our fate
So slowly murmurs through its rock-bound cave.
Ever the tide returns; but now at ebb,
When the white sands gleam bare and nothing
    stirs
Save the salt seaweed fringe of little streams
That trickle from lone pools o'er the dented sand.
Cannot I, as the mariner, recline,
Waiting the longed-for hour when with a stir
Of soft, delicious fragrance from the deep,
And heavenly alternations in the kiss
Of the sea-breeze, elastic as young hopes,
The swelling waters hasten, and his bark
At last floats off, rising so steadily,
Her sails all filling with that sweet surprise,
Till her bright keel cuts sharply the green floor,
And tosses off the billows till they laugh.

Yet must we wait, whose voyage knows no content,
Whose compass turns within the eternal stars—
A voyage beyond illimitable worlds;
Yet must I pause upon this earthly ebb,
And play and smile at care and soothe the pain,
Until the raven hair of misery shines.

Brave be thy heart, O sailor of the world!
Erect thy vision, strong and resolute.
Let disappointments strike, and leaden days
Visit thee like a snowdrift across flowers;
Be calm and truthful, and outcheer thy pangs.
And, when thou sufferest, learn from all thy woes,
Those faithful teachers who shall spell thee all
Hope's alphabet and Bible lore.   Be calm—
Even in a little this rude voyage is done.
Then heave the time-stained anchor, trim thy sails,
And o'er the bosom of the untrammelled deep
Ride in the heavenly boat and touch new stars.

MURILLO'S MAGDALEN

HER eyes are fixed; they seek the skies.
   Was earth so low? Was life so vain?
Was Time such weary sacrifice?
   This hopeless task, this eating pain?

Smooth, smooth the tresses of thy hair;
   Release that cold, contracted brow!
I have not lived without despair;
   Look down on me—some mercy show!

I cannot bear those silent skies;
   The weight is pressing in my heart;
Life is eternal sacrifice,
   The livelong hour, the selfish smart.

I wake to tears, in tears I close
   The weary eyes so fixed above;
I cannot see the skies of rose,
   My heavy tresses will not move.

Hope cannot heal my breaking heart,
  Heaven will not lift my dread despair;
I need another soul to part
  These brows of steel and join in prayer.

Sails there no bark on life's wild sea
  That bears a soul whose faith has set,
Who may renew my light in me,
  And both shall thus the past forget?

SLEEPY HOLLOW

(1855)

This poem was written at Mr. Emerson's request, for singing at the consecration of the Concord cemetery where his ashes now repose. But
finding it could not easily be sung by the village choir, Mr. Emerson
desired me to write an ode that could be sung — which was done.— F. B. S.

NO abbeys gloom, no dark cathedral stoops,
   No winding torches paint the midnight air;
Here the green pine delights, the aspen droops
   Along the modest pathways—and those fair,
Pale asters of the season spread their plumes
Around this field, fit garden for our tombs.

Here shalt thou pause to hear the funeral bell
   Slow stealing o'er thy heart in this calm place;
Not with a throb of pain, a feverish knell,
   But in its kind and supplicating grace
It says: "Go, Pilgrim, on thy march! be more
Friend to the friendless than thou wast before."

Learn from the loved one's rest, serenity;
   To-morrow that soft bell for thee shall sound,
And thou repose beneath the whispering tree,
   One tribute more to this submissive ground.
Prison thy soul from malice—bar out pride—
Nor these pale flowers nor this still field deride!

Rather to those ascents of Being turn
  Where a ne'er-setting sun illumes the year
Eternal ; and the incessant watch-fires burn
  Of unspent holiness and goodness clear ;
Forget man's littleness —deserve the best—
God's mercy in thy thought and life confest.

THE NEW ENGLAND FARM-HOUSE

IN CANTON, MASSACHUSETTS

METHINKS I see the hilltops round me swell,
And meadow vales that kiss their tawny
  brooks,
And fawn the glittering sands that hug the grass,
Old valleys shorn by farmers numerous years,
Some mossy orchards murmuring with perfume,
And our red farm-house. What a wreck that
  was!—
Its rotten shingles peeling 'fore the winds
When roaring March fell in the offshore breeze;
The kitchen, with its salt-box full of eggs,
And Taylor's *Holy Living* on the lid.
Our parlor kept its buffet rarely oped—
Much did I wonder at yon glassy doors,
And stacks of crockery sublimely piled—
Hills of blue plates, and teapots sere with age;
And spoons, old silver, tiniest of that breed.
It was a sacred place, and, save I whisked
Sometimes a raisin or a seed-cake thence,
With furtive glance I scanned the curious spot.
The curtains at the windows kept all dark;
Green paper was the compound; and the floor,

Well scrubbed, showed its vacuities, content
With modest subterfuge of mats (the work
Of some brave aunt, industrious as a fly),
And interwove of rags, yet such to me
I hardly dared intrude on them my shoe.

TRURO, ON CAPE COD

OFT would I tread that far-off, quiet shore,
And sit allayed with its unnoticed store.
What though nor fame nor hope my fancy fired,
Nor aught of that to which my youth aspired,
Nor woman's beauty, nor her friendly cheer,
That nourish life like some soft atmosphere!
For here I found I was a welcome guest
At generous Nature's hospitable feast.
The barren moors no fences girdled high,—
These endless beaches planting might defy,—
And the blue sea admitted all the air—
A cordial draught, so sparkling and so rare.

While there I wandered,—far and wide between,—
Proud of my salt expanse and country clean.
A few old fishers seemed my only men,
Some aged wives their queens, not seen till then;
Those had outsailed the wild, o'er-heaving seas,
These closely nestled in their old roof-trees.
Too dull to mark, they eyed me without harm;
Careless of alms, I was not their alarm.
The aged widow in her cottage lone,
Of solitude and musing patient grown,
Could let me wander o'er her scanty fields,
And pick the flower that contemplation yields.

Oft had she sat the winter storms away,
And feared the sea, and trembled at its play ;
Noticed the clouds, and guessed when storms were
    nigh ;
Like me, alone, far from humanity.

Her straw all plaited and her day's work done,
There as she sat she saw the reddening sun
Drop o'er the distant cape, and felt that May
Had outbid April for a sweeter day,
And dreamed of flowers and garden-work to do,
And half resolved, and half it kept in view.

This census o'er, and all the rest was mine.
The gliding vessel on the horizon's line,
That left the world wherein my fancy strayed,
Yet long enough her soft good-by delayed
To let my eye engross her beauty rare,
Kissed by the seas and mistress of the air.
That, too, was mine—the green and curling wave,
Child of the sand—a playful child and brave ;
Urged by the breeze, the crashing surges fall—
Let zephyrs dance—and silken bubbles all ;
But let the gale lift from yon Eastern realm—
No more the ship perceives the patient helm ;
Tranced in the tumbling roar she whirls away,
A shattered ghost, a chip for thy dread play.

TRURO, ON CAPE COD

Wild ocean wave! some eyes look out o'er thee
And fill with tears, and ask, Could such things be!
Why slept the All-seeing Eye when death was
   near!
Be hushed each doubt, assuage each troubled fear!
Think One who made the sea and made the wind
May also feel for our poor humankind;
And they who sleep amid the surges tall
Summoned great Nature to their funeral,
And she obeyed. We fall not far from shore;
The seabird's wail, the skies our fates deplore;
The melancholy main goes sounding on
His world-old anthem o'er our horizon.

TRURO

A REGRET

THE vain regret, the foolish, wasted tear,
  Old memories, and most my thought of thee—
Why will they rise and darkly haunt me here,
    Whilst the gay blackbird whistles o'er the lea,
    And water-lilies shine, and the blue sea
I little dream of, yonder o'er the hill?
    Alas for Hope! since not again to me
Thy form shall rise, thy life my being thrill—
Gone as thou art—gone and forever still.

Forgive this weak lament! and still forgive
  In our past days a foolish, erring man!
And yet that I was true thou must believe—
    An empty heart that with thy life o'erran,
    Creature of beauty—Nature's rarest plan!
So beautiful, who would not love thee near?
    We are not carved in stone. The day that ran
Our passion into form why should we fear?
Nor more that silent Past, closed save to some
        cold tear.

Then bloomed the flowers along Life's sandy waste,
  The waters sparkled in the glancing sun,
144

TRURO

And Fate for thee prepared with eager haste
  The festive measure—sorrowful to one
  Who on thy beauty gazed, but could not run
To slake his thirst at that unfathomed spring;
  But feverish looked, and only looked upon,
  While Nature hastened with her queenly ring
And crowned thee fairest—her most charming
    thing.

Why must we live? why pause upon this shore?
  Its cold despair our flying souls must chill;
And, sitting lone, I hear the ocean's roar,
  While most subdued my heart and wish and will—
  Like its unsounded depths my hopes are still;
A moment I may pause, and ask the Past,
  Since in the Present frozen is Life's rill,
Had she no joys that might their sunshine cast
On these Siberian wastes and slippery glaciers
    vast?

Though beauty smile not on a wasted heart,
  And with the years I must my lot deplore,
Though Love be distant,—Life an actor's part,
  One moment moored, then sailing off the
    shore,—
  Still, while thy thought remains, I weep no more;
For in thy sweet yet artless dignity,
  Thy polished mind, in Youth's unlearned lore,

There yet remains a happiness for me,
And thee I still remember, Rosalie!
Where went thou straying, when the heart was
    young,
  And green the leaf swayed on Life's bending
    tree?
When the eye saw, and nimbly sped the tongue
  To tell of stream and bird and heaving sea—
  And human fate glowed for eternity?
Then Hope on high poised her romantic scroll
  Where poets' years are writ—not the cold plea
For having lived : as the long surges roll
Across my years, now but my knell they toll.

THE PORTRAITS

I. JULIA

JULIA—at her name my mind
  Throws its griefs and cares behind :
She, the love of early years,
Smiling through her childish tears—
Julia! child of love and pain,
One I ne'er shall see again.

And forgive me, Julia dear,
For the sins of that long year!
Think of me with kindly thought,
And condemn me not for naught.

By thine eyes, so softly brown,
By the light and glistening crown
That so gently o'er thy head
Did its shining lustre shed ;
By that sad yet loving mouth,
Rose of fragrance from the South ;
By thy form, oh, lovelier far
Than a seraph's from a star ;
By that ankle small and neat,
And thy little twinkling feet ;—

147

I must still thy loss deplore,
Since the fatal hour sped o'er
When we parted, ne'er to meet,
On the silent noontide street.

Should I live a thousand years,
    I cannot forget thee,—never,—
Nor the hot and weary tears
    That I shed, from thee to sever;
Never will thy truthful eyes
Leave me, in this world of lies.

Girl of love and graceful youth,
Girl all beauty, girl all truth!
Spirit clad in purer air
Than Time's hateful fashions wear!
Angel, shining through my dreams
When Youth, Hope, and Joy were themes!
Dead seems all Youth's memory,
Save one thought—the thought of thee.

From the blossoms of the Spring
Beauty wreathed thee in her ring;
From the airs of dewy skies
Melted sadness in those eyes—
Speechless, soft and fearful glances,
Maidenhood's enamoured trances—
Faintly trembling, dimly felt,
With a name not aptly spelt.

THE PORTRAITS

Now, the moods of passion over,
I am loved by none, nor lover;
'T was not thus when Julia's eye
To my own made sweet reply.
Orphan from her earliest years,
Cradled on a couch of tears,
Dark as Winter's dreariest night
Was her lot—yet she was light;
Never closed her feeling's spring,
Faithful life's best offering.

" Time shall never wile me more
On its dark, its frowning shore."
So felt I for Julia's fate,
Like my own, most desolate;
Years of pain, those years all sorrow,
To-day wretched as to-morrow;
Never finished, never fast,
Falling slowly to the Past—
What a youth was this to me,
Born for love and sympathy!

There was sorrow in her air,
Sweetness married to despair,
In her mouth, that would have laughed
And Love's ruby vintage quaffed;
In her softly shaded cheek,
Where Love could his vengeance wreak;

In her sweet, entrancing eye,
Whence Love's arrows sought to fly:
Could, then, Fortune frame a creature
Perfect so in every feature?
Beauteous as the dove's soft wing,
Or a fountain of the Spring,
Or the sunset as it sinks,
While the Night its radiance drinks
For a glowing beverage,
Necta of Day's purple age:
Could Fortune, mocking her, declare
Lovely Julia to despair?
Such dark mystery is life,
This debate 'twixt sleep and strife.

But thy heart grew never old!
Naught was there save sunset's gold,
Crimson evenings, blushing mornings,
And all Nature's wise adornings.

Where art fled ne'er have I heard;
In this earthly state? No word.
Art still near the wide blue river
That beyond the meads doth quiver?
Or beneath yon mountain's shade,
By the murmuring chestnut glade?
Shadow of departed years,
Draped in Beauty, draped in Tears,

150

THE PORTRAITS

Where, across life's shadowy main,
Child of sweetness, child of pain!
Art thou drifting, then, to-day?
Dearest Julia, to me say!

II. GRACE

GRACE was perfect, fresh, and fair,
Cheerful as a mountain air;
Blithely fearless, glad and free,
Pouting lips, with hazel ee.
O'er her firm-set figure played
Charms to make a saint afraid;
To this magnet strong and sweet
Swift my willing steps must fleet.
Grace was all a paragon—
Oh, she drew me like a sun!

Round about her valley lie
Purple mountains on the sky,
And within her valley's fold
Lakes that set no price in gold,
Tracks that climb the crag and glen,
And a race of frugal men.

Buoyant, wilful, frank, and gay,
Grace ne'er lived a wretched day—
Joy of parents, loved by all,
Warmed and cheered her father's hall.

151

Years of sadness now thrown over,
Once again was I a lover;
Laughed again the lake's low shore,
Laughed the hilltops ten times more,
And the birches in the wood
Fluttered midst the solitude.
"Grace was lovely, Grace was fine—
Could not Grace, dear Grace, be mine!"

Many times around my light,
Darting at the centre bright,
Have I viewed a wretched moth
Singe his feather, by my troth.
I had wept and I had loved—
Frail and fatal all it proved;
Might have known it ne er could be—
Might have guessed she ha.ed me!

Girl of Life's determined hours,
Clad in glory as the flowers,
Virginal as Venus came
From the sea at Morning's flame,
All a sunny, fond surprise,
With her wealth of hazel eyes—
She was not, if I was, poor,—
Parents prudent,—life in store,—
Could I sing her virtues more?

THE PORTRAITS

Grace had beauty, Grace had truth—
Well I loved her in my youth!
And she taught me a fine word—
This (I might have elsewhere heard):
That not all I wish is mine—
What I have should seem divine.

III. MADELINE

MANY days have never made
Me forget that oak's green shade
Under which, in Autumn fair,
While October gilt the air,
Madeline was musing lone
On a cold and mossy stone.
Below her feet the river ran
Like the fleeting hopes of Man;
Around, the unshorn grasses high,
O'er her head the deep blue sky;
Best of all was Madeline,
Gypsy figure, tall and fine.
Yes, and she was Nature's child:
Airs and skies to her were mild;
Never breeze her thoughts perturbed,
Never storm her cheek disturbed.

In her skiff she glided o'er
Foaming crests that swiftly bore
Her to the many-wooded shore;

In her bark, far o'er the tide,
Madeline would smoothly glide
On the wild and whirling wave,
In blasts that 'gainst the islands rave,
Madeline swept 'neath the sky—
Born of Nature, but more high.

Child of grace, to Nature dear,
Be the sky her broad compeer!
Lists her song the sighing wood,
Where she like a statue stood,
But with low and heartfelt voice
That could bid my soul rejoice;
Be her light yon star so keen,
Pure and distant, Heaven's Queen;
Let the sea, the boundless sea,
Her perpetual anthem be,
While the gray gull wets his wing
To the green waves' murmuring,
And the white beach lines the shore
In its sandy curvature.

Sinful cities not in her
Could a feeble passion stir;
Filled with love, her lyric eye
Gave its figure to the sky;
Like a lyre, her heart obeyed
Whispers of the forest shade,

154

THE PORTRAITS

Buds she sang, and fresh spring flowers,
Birds that carolled in her bowers,
And the lonely, sorrowing sea,
Still she sang its lullaby.

Slave to each impulsive hour,
How could I resist her power?
Or not kneel and worship there,
When she tinged the Autumn air
With her joy or with her pain—
Lit the chill October rain
O'er the low and sullen hill
(Outlined, if the hour were still,
By some leaden cloud behind)
With its scanty grasses lined,
Serely russet, as the day,
Hermit-like, went out in gray.[1]

Muse of the Island, pure and free!
Spirit of the sapphire sea!
How can I forget the time
We went wandering in our prime,
And beneath the tall pine-trees
Felt the tearful Autumn breeze?

[1] This passage shows a clear reminiscence of the happy days at Curzon's Mill, and that region where young Channing spent so much time, and where the best of his early poems were written. These portraits are much idealized, but traces of several of his youthful friends may be found in them. The Julia afterward mentioned as buried in Plymouth was a different person; but possibly an earlier Julia was the Sibylla of *The Wanderer.*

Hope had I of lofty fame
To embalm a poet's name,
In some grandly festive measure
Fitliest for a nation's pleasure :
Thus it was I dreamed at first—
Madeline ! thy beauty nursed
In me finer thought and feeling,
To myself my heart revealing.

Ghost of wishes dead and gone,
Haunting hopes still limping on,—
Echoes from a sunken land
Falling on a desert strand,—
Cold content and broken plan—
Still the boy lives in the man !

IV. CONSTANTIA

BEST of all Constantia proved—
Best of all her truth I loved ;
Free as air and fixed as Fate,
Fitted for a hero's mate.
Beauty dear Constantia had,
Fit to make a lover mad ;
Every grace she 'd gently turn
Strong to do and swift to learn ;
Truthful as the twilight sky
Was her melting, lustrous eye—

THE PORTRAITS

Full of sweetness as the South
Was her firm and handsome mouth.

Child of conscience, child of truth,—
Treasures far outlasting youth,—
Would my verse had but the power
Again to shape that brightest hour
When beneath the shadowy tree
First I pressed the hand of thee!
While the sighing summer wind
Toned its murmur through the mind,
And the moon shined clear above,
Smiling chaste, like those we love.

I can ne'er be loved again
As I was on that sweet plain,
Though I sigh for fourscore years,
Watering all Earth's sands with tears.
I am old—my life is sere;
Beauty never can appear
As it was when I was young,
Love and joy upon my tongue.
Give me Passion, give me Youth!
More than all, oh, give me Truth!
Let the beauties steal my heart
In their deep, entrancing art—
Yet the safer shalt thou prove,
Dear Constantia! in my love.

How the feverish glances fly
Off the dark, the laughing eye!
Mark the brown and braided hair,
To weak hearts a fearful snare.
I have seen the Southern skies
Shut their soft, love-laden eyes,
Seen the floor of those calm seas
Rippled by the orange-breeze;
But I fled such azure dreams
For thy frozen Northern streams.

If my heart is growing old,
Thine is neither worn nor cold;
If my life has lost its flower,
Thine still wears its crimson dower,
And the early morning beam
Pulsates on its golden stream.

May a cold, sepulchral breeze
Every feeling in me freeze,
Stab me through and through with pain,
If I ever love again!
More—let all the Graces go,
And the Muses thickly sow
Harsh and crabbèd seed all o'er
Helicon's harmonious shore,—
Subtle Venus snap her zone,
Phœbus carve me into stone,—

THE PORTRAITS

If I leave Constantia's side !
My joy and hope, my peace, my pride.

V. EMERSON

(1857)

HERE sometimes gliding in nis peaceful skiff
Climéné sails, heir of the world, and notes
In his perception, that no thing escapes,
Each varying pulse along Life's arteries—
Both what she half resolves and half effects,
As well as her whole purpose. To his eye
The silent stars of many a midnight heaven
Have beamed tokens of love, types of the Soul,
And lifted him to more primeval natures.
In those far-moving barks on heaven's sea
Radiates of force he saw ; and while he moved
From man, on the eternal billow, still his heart
Beat with some natural fondness for his race.

In other lands they might have worshipped him ;
Nations had stood and blocked their chariot wheels
At his approach—towns stooped beneath his foot !
But here, in our vast wilderness, he walks
Alone—if 't is to be alone when stars
And breath of summer mountain airs and morn
And the wild music of the untempered sea
Consort with human genius.

Oh, couldst not thou revere, bold stranger (prone
Inly to smile and chide at human power),
Our humble fields and lowly stooping hills,
When thou shalt learn that here Climéné trod!

VI. THOREAU

(1857)

I SEE Rudolpho cross our honest fields,
Collapsed with thought, cool as the Stagirite
At intellectual problems; mastering
Day after day part of the world's concern;
Still adding to his list beetle and bee—
Of what the Vireo builds a pensile nest,
And why the Peetweet drops her giant egg
In wheezing meadows odorous with sweet brake.
Nor welcome dawns nor shrinking nights him
    menace,
Still girt about for observation, yet
Keen to pursue the devious lanes that lead
To knowledge oft so dearly bought.

Who wonders that the flesh declines to grow
Along his sallow pits; or that his life,
To social pleasure careless, pines away
In dry seclusion and unfruitful shade?
Martyr! for eye too sharp and ear too fine!
I must admire thy brave apprenticeship

THE PORTRAITS

To these dry forages, although the worldling
Laugh in his sleeve at thy compelled devotion,
And would declare an accidental stroke
Surpassed whole eons of Rudolpho's file.
Yet shalt thou learn, Rudolpho, as thou walkst,
More from the winding lanes where Nature leaves
Her unaspiring creatures, and surpass
In some fine saunter her declivity.

VII. ROSALBA

With thee, fathomless Ocean, that dear child
I link—a summer child, flower of the world,
Rosalba! for, like thee, she has no bound
Or limit to her beauty; Venus-zoned,
She rather, like thy billows, bends with grace.
Nor deem the Grecian fable all a myth,
That Aphrodite from a shell appeared,
Soft spanned upon the wave; for o'er thy heart,
Unheeding stranger! thus Rosalba falls,
And by one entrance on thy privacy
Unrolls the mysteries and gives them tongue.

Child of the poet's thought! if ever God
Made any creature that could thee surpass,—
The lightest sunset cloud that purpling swims
Across the zenith's lake,—the foam of seas,—
The roses when they paint the green sand-wastes

Of our remotest Cape,—or the hour near dawn,—
I cannot fathom it; nor how thou art made :
How these attempered elements in the mass
Run to confusion and exhale in fault,—
Begetting monstrous passions and dark thoughts,
Or slow contriving malice, or cold spite,
Or leagues of dulness, self-persuaded rare,—
But rise in thee like the vast Ocean's grace,
Ne'er to be bounded by my heart or hope,
Yet ever decorous, modest, and complete.

Rose on her cheeks, are roses in her heart,
And softer on the earth her footstep falls
Than earliest twilight airs across the wave ;
While in her heart the unfathomed sea of love
Its never-ceasing tide pours onward.

VIII.   A HOUSEHOLD FRIEND
(December 15, 1866)

If the winter skies be o'er us,
And the winter months before us,
When the tempest, Boreal falling,
Hurls his icy bolts appalling,
Let us yet thy soul inherit,
Equable and nice in spirit !
Whom in turbulent December
With still peace we can remember.

162

THE PORTRAITS

Muses should thy birthday reckon
As to one their foretastes beckon;
Who in thought and action never
Could the right from self dissever;
Taken with no serpent charming,
By no tyranny's alarming;
In thy sure conviction better
Than in blurred Tradition's fetter;
Would the State such souls might cherish,
And her liberties ne'er perish!

Age must dart no frost to harm thee,
Fell reverses ne'er alarm thee,
Having that within thy being
Still the good in evil seeing;
Faithful heart and faithful doing
Bring Life's forces humbly suing.

Now we bid the dear Penates
(Inward guardians with whom Fate is)
And the Lar, whose altar flaming
From thy household merits naming,
And Vertumnus we solicit,
Whose return brings no deficit,
Bacchus with his ivy thyrses,
And Pomona's friendly verses,
Or what other joys may be
Pouring from Antiquity:

Let them o'er thy roof, displaying
Happiest stars, stand brightly raying!

In thy thought poetic splendor
This late age spontaneous render,
Shed o'er acts of love divine,
Fit for thee and fit for thine!

IX. SYBILLA

In the proud mansion on the city street,
Strewed with the loans of luxury, that Time
Wafts down o'erpowering from the burdened
    Past—
Homeless and hopeless in those cruel walls
Sybilla went—her heart long since bereaved.
She heard the footfalls sear the crowded streets,—
Her fatal birthright,—where no human pulse
To hers was beating; there she shunned the day!

Tall churches and rich houses draped in flowers,
And lovely maids tricked out with pearls and gold,
Barbaric pomp! and crafty usurers bent—
All passed she by, the terror in her soul;
Then sped she on her flight—a reindeer-course.
Day's dying light painted the quiet fields,
The pale green sky reflected in their pools,—

THE PORTRAITS

A soft, clear light,—and in that heaven afar
O'er emerald waters glowed the evening star.
Oh, why was Earth so fair! was love so fond
Ever consumed within its ring of fire!

X.   JULIA OF PLYMOUTH

SOCIAL and warm the ruddy curtains fall
Around the dreamy casements; till the roar
Of the continuous surf upon the ledge
That shores the ocean's ingress, whispering lulls,
And Fancy brings the forms of other days.

O loved and gone! the darling of our hearts,
With thy soft, winning ways, caressing smiles,
And step more light than tracks the forest fawn;
Who taught the old how kind the young might be!
How often thy slight figure, wandering o'er
The breezy lawn, or couched within the shade,
Made sweeter music than all sounds beside!

Gone—oh, forever gone! alone she sleeps
    Upon the hillside looking o'er the sea;
Alone! when every heart, full of thy worth,
    Enchanting Julia! sends its love to thee!

EPITHALAMIUM

(1862)

FRIEND! in thy new relation
　There is no provocation
　For Thought's demise;
Be all more nobly brave!
Assist each slave,
And yet more share
Thy hours and thoughts and care
　　With others,
　　Thy kinsmen and thy brothers!
　　And more a patriot be
　　Through Love's wise chemistry!

Long have I watched thee rule
Thyself; and if a still
And lustrous guardian school
　　Thee to a stiller patience now,
　　In this dear vow,
　　And nearer to the stars
　　(Save that all-reddening Mars),
More consonant with the train
Of evening and sweet Hesperus,
　　And her who walks the night,
　　In blushing radiance strayed,

166

EPITHALAMIUM

A well-proportioned light,
  A sea-born maid,
Who from old Ocean's foam
Laughed, and made men at home;

In truth, if this prove so,—
    If her soft beams
    Silver the rushing streams,
    And gild the moss
Where the ancestral brothers toss—
Dark oaks and murmuring pines,
Stags of a thousand tines;
    These rocks so grave, if they
    Smile with humected day,
    And silken zephyrs thrill
The maple's foliage, where the bird
    Rose-breasted rings
    With Music's clearest springs,—
      What then!
    Though softer, we 're still men!

TO-MORROW AND TO-MORROW AND
TO-MORROW

TO-MORROW comes? dost say, my Friend,
  " To-morrow "?
Far down below those pines the sunset flings,
Long arching o'er, its lines of ruddy light;
And the wind murmurs little harmonies,
And underneath their wings the tender birds
Droop their averted heads—silent their song.

But not a word whispers the moaning wind—
Not when in faint array the primal stars
Trail with the banners of the unfurled Night;
Nor even when the low-hung moon just glints,
And faintly, with few touches, sears the wood;
  Not there, not then, doth Nature idly say,
  Nor whisper idly of another day;
  That other morn itself its morrow is;
  That other day shall see no shade of this.

168

THE ICE RAVINE

NEVER was the sight more gay:
   Down the rapid water flows;
Deep the ravine's rondelay,
   Stealing up the silent snows.
Like an organ's carved woodwork,
   Richly waxed, the ice-tubes stand;
In them hidden stops do lurk,
   And I see the Master's hand.

Swift his fingers strike the keys,
   Glittering all with rings of light;
Bubbles break, and, born with ease,
   Sparkle constant, swift, and bright;
Now upon the rocks the roar
   Of the streamlet beats the bass,
Deeply murmuring through the floor
   Of sparse snow and frozen grass.

Red as ruby wine the hue
   Of this running brook, that brings
Through the ice ravine this true
   Music for the native kings.

Solemn stands the Ash-tree near,
 Not one leaf upon his crown;
Still the Barberry, still the clear
 Landscape of the meadows brown.

Thus they listen every day;
 Wind may roar, and rain may run;
Clear or dull, the streamlet's play
 Sounds that music—All in One.

MEMORIES OF FANNY McGREGOR

This poem recalls a voyage down Boston Harbor in company with Miss McGregor during the Civil War. She was, not long after, accidentally shot near Franconia, in the New Hampshire mountain-land. A person of great beauty and wit, perhaps exalted poetically in this tribute.

WE felt the shadows build the Fort,
   And touch Cohassett's withering hills;
The breeze that cooled our Boston port
   Ran fresh, as leap the mountain rills
Down gray Franconia's hoary woods,
Saved from the axe, dear solitudes.

The sky's deep blue adorned the Flag,
   That pathos of our nation's cause,
Battled in blood from sea to crag,
   For home and hearth, for life and laws:
Lovelier than all, a woman's heart,
Reflecting all, and taking part.

How void the play still Nature makes
   Where thrills no breast with human fear!
Dull sets that sun—no wavelet breaks
   Till woman's loveliness appear;
Heat of the light we coldly bear,
The radiant of Time's atmosphere.

171

O lovely day that died so soon,
   Live long in Her, more fairly planned!
And like the sea when shines the moon,
   Reflecting in its ebb the hand
Inscrutable that flings the star,
Thy beauty leads my thoughts afar.

To thee respond the dancing waves,
   To thee the grace-encircled shore,
Whose lonely sands old Ocean laves
   And pebbles bright flows lisping o'er;
Thy tranquil heart was ever bent
In beauty to be eloquent.

From envious skies thy star shines down,
   Not unacquainted with its place;
They wreathe for thee an angel's crown,
   And gem the virtues of thy face.
Ah, fated shot! devoid of power
O'er her whose beauty was her dower!
  .   .   .   .

Called from the voice of life, the tasks of pain,
   Thine eye no more the rounding day shalt see
In sunlit hours or chill and sobbing rain;
   Nor we hear trace of old-time melody
That told in music of another shore,
Where rests Time's mournful wave, ne'er breaking
   more.

THE LATE-FOUND FRIEND

(1901)

ALL, all had long-time gone;
  On Earth's wide bound I wandered lone,
By sweeping waves, whose glittering tides
Once safely o'er, no sailor rides—
When out of that soft greensward shore
I saw a vessel steer once more,
And at her prow a tall, straight form;
'T was Margaret, poised so high above Earth's
    storm!

Simple and sweet she surely is
  As opening dawn or day's last look;
Within her heart, within her eyes,
  Meet all the charms of mead and brook,
When rings amid the open fields
  That dear, delightful strain along—
Great Nature's heart in little birds,
  Piping their unmaterial song.

Late in the deep and dying night,
  When sounds are still, and frozen the moor,
There echoes, far from human plight,
  The cottage curs' unceasing roar;

Then, in that strange funereal pall
   That veils the Earth and hides the skies,
I seem to hear a note that falls
   Sweeter than tidings of surprise.

I need not ask—I do not stay;
   'T is Margaret's voice—no other sound
Could ever wake a rondelai
   Within this heart by Sorrow bound.

"Wanderer of pain! I am a truth to be
   For those I stoop to, mercy to implore;
   A certain lighthouse on Earth's murky shore;
O God! I kneel and ask that those in me
May trust their heart's best love implicitly—
   Trust and believe—see in my soul their own,
   As one sweet viol clears another's tone."

   So from the drooping skies
   The quicker lightning flies,
And makes our shadowed hearts bright 'neath
     those lovely eyes.
For whom now would you raise the tower of
     Scorn?
Now when yon azure distances, upborne
In their far-shadowed folds of ruby light,
Pale and grow gloomy as the wondrous Night
Pours forth her stream of stars o'er Heaven's
     deep sea,
And mocks our wandering, far Futurity.

THE SAGE

(EMERSON)

(1897)

WHEN I was young I knew a sage—
A man *he* was of middle age;
Clear was his mind as forest brooks,
And reams of wisdom in his looks.

But if I asked this sage-like man
Questions of wisdom in *my* plan,
Faintly the smile shed o'er his face,
A beam of joy, a smile of grace.

The answer that I needed bad
Ne'er reached my ear, nor gay nor sad;
"That might be so," the sage would say,
Exactly flat as mere " Good day."

Within his mind there seemed to be
A fixed reserve, a pleasant lea:
"Not I—I cannot mend your state,"
To Yes, to No, inveterate.

To all alike he charming was;
His words were wise in Virtue's cause;
Distinct, clear-minded—old and young
Upon his words in rapture hung.

"Come to my woods, come to my fields!
There Nature her revision yields;
These things were made to be enjoyed—
Great is the pleasure, great the reward.

"Unnumbered shine the nightly flowers,
To man the wonder of his hours;
The heavens themselves invite his gaze,
Those actors in their native plays."

Forth went he, armed, to see the world;
Love was his weapon—joy it hurled;
Yet ne'er a word he spoke of them—
Silent, yet shining like a gem.

WELCOME TO THEE NOT GONE

(A TRIBUTE TO MARSTON WATSON, WRITTEN IN 1899)

FRIEND of my early years! friend of my hours
 Fast fading from these shores, from Time's
  dim bowers!
The same to-day,—e'er living in my mind,—
Sweet, thoughtful, tender, patient to thy kind—
Marston, I would not weep that thou art gone,
Leaving me hapless on these shores alone;
Dear Heart, I will not grieve, since God allowed
So vast a tribute and a soul so proud;
Since thou wert sent to teach me to forget,
By these low shores where my poor voyage was
  set,
These steep obliquities that shade my path,
While thy far-reaching view o'ergoes their
  wrath.

Marston! I see thee still—that far-off look
Away, across the skies, the ever-rolling brook,
Or that dark, troubled Sea among the isles;
The breeze blows up; the flowers, the heavens,
  all smiles.
Smiling we take our way across the tombs,
Stand on the hilltop, hear the rushing looms

In the long valley nestling at our feet;
Scan the vast basin where the heavens meet
Their own blue pageant, sent from skies to greet;
Marston delights in all—or sandy reach,
Or sparkling billows on the Gurnet beach;
The poorest weed, the smallest fly that waves,
To him the same as the great Heroes' graves.

"I am not gone; I live—I 'm with thee still!
I stand off-looking from the windy hill
With thee; 't is just the same; weep not for me!
I murmur in the breeze, I sail upon the sea;
I see with far-off look the westering sun
Play o'er the oak-groves when the day is done.
No, not a tear! let us be cheerful now!
I am not dead—why, what a thought! my vow
Was always sped to life; in Death's lone camp
I do not walk alone; I have my lamp,
My steadfast light, burning from ancient shades,
Eternal remnants from prophetic glades.

"The breezes fan my cheek; I am not dead;
My soul has only waved its wings and fled
From these low-hanging equinoctial storms;
Hail, Heaven and life! hail, gods and sempiternal
    forms!"

The Romantic Tradition in American Literature

An Arno Press Collection

Alcott, A. Bronson, editor. **Conversations with Children on the Gospels.** Boston, 1836/1837. Two volumes in one.

Bartol, C[yrus] A. **Discourses on the Christian Spirit and Life.** 2nd edition. Boston, 1850.

Boker, George H[enry]. **Poems of the War.** Boston, 1864.

Brooks, Charles T. **Poems, Original and Translated.** Selected and edited by W. P. Andrews. Boston, 1885.

Brownell, Henry Howard. **War-Lyrics** and Other Poems. Boston, 1866.

Brownson, O[restes] A. **Essays and Reviews Chiefly on Theology, Politics, and Socialism.** New York, 1852.

Channing, [William] Ellery (The Younger). **Poems.** Boston, 1843.

Channing, [William] Ellery (The Younger). **Poems of Sixty-Five Years.** Edited by F. B. Sanborn. Philadelphia and Concord, 1902.

Chivers, Thomas Holley. **Eonchs of Ruby:** A Gift of Love. New York, 1851.

Chivers, Thomas Holley. **Virginalia;** or, Songs of My Summer Nights. (Reprinted from *Research Classics,* No. 2, 1942). Philadelphia, 1853.

Cooke, Philip Pendleton. **Froissart Ballads,** and Other Poems. Philadelphia, 1847.

Cranch, Christopher Pearse. **The Bird and the Bell,** with Other Poems. Boston, 1875.

[Dall], Caroline W. Healey, editor. **Margaret and Her Friends.** Boston, 1895.

[D'Arusmont], Frances Wright. **A Few Days in Athens.** Boston, 1850.

Everett, Edward. **Orations and Speeches,** on Various Occasions. Boston, 1836.

Holland, J[osiah] G[ilbert]. **The Marble Prophecy,** and Other Poems. New York, 1872.

Huntington, William Reed. **Sonnets and a Dream.** Jamaica, N. Y., 1899.

Jackson, Helen [Hunt]. **Poems.** Boston, 1892.

Miller, Joaquin (Cincinnatus Hiner Miller). **The Complete Poetical Works of Joaquin Miller.** San Francisco, 1897.

Parker, Theodore. **A Discourse of Matters Pertaining to Religion.** Boston, 1842.

Pinkney, Edward C. **Poems.** Baltimore, 1838.

Reed, Sampson. **Observations on the Growth of the Mind.** *Including,* **Genius** (Reprinted from *Aesthetic Papers,* Boston, 1849). 5th edition. Boston, 1859.

Sill, Edward Rowland. **The Poetical Works of Edward Rowland Sill.** Boston and New York, 1906.

Simms, William Gilmore. **Poems:** Descriptive, Dramatic, Legendary and Contemplative. New York, 1853. Two volumes in one.

Simms, William Gilmore, editor. **War Poetry of the South.** New York, 1866.

Stickney, Trumbull. **The Poems of Trumbull Stickney.** Boston and New York, 1905.

Timrod, Henry. **The Poems of Henry Timrod.** Edited by Paul H. Hayne. New York, 1873.

Trowbridge, John Townsend. **The Poetical Works of John Townsend Trowbridge.** Boston and New York, 1903.

Very, Jones. **Essays and Poems.** [Edited by R. W. Emerson]. Boston, 1839.

Very, Jones. **Poems and Essays.** Boston and New York, 1886.

White, Richard Grant, editor. **Poetry:** Lyrical, Narrative, and Satirical of the Civil War. New York, 1866.

Wilde, Richard Henry. **Hesperia:** A Poem. Edited by His Son (William Wilde). Boston, 1867.

Willis, Nathaniel Parker. **The Poems, Sacred, Passionate, and Humorous, of Nathaniel Parker Willis.** New York, 1868.